Mark Dever and Greg Gilbert are two of my favorite preachers. They both believe the Bible says something eternally important for every person. The Lord has gifted Dever to make me think about what the Bible says. The Lord has gifted Gilbert to make me see or visualize what the Bible says. This book combines both of those gifts to help us preachers and listeners think about and visualize "good preaching." I'm so thankful they've teamed up to give us this readable, to-the-point, theologically sound, practical, and inspiring book on preaching.

—Thabiti Anyabwile, pastor
First Baptist Church, Grand Cayman

Worshipful, intellectually rich, humble and humorous, this book was a delight to read. Gilbert and Dever make a strong case for the recovery of the centrality of the preached word in the church. Preaching is not the church's job; it is the church's life. Full of great insight and practical wisdom, I wish every pastor would immerse himself in this book.

—J.D. Greear, lead pastor, The Summit Church, Raleigh-Durham, North Carolina and author of *Gospel: Recovering the Power that Made Christianity Revolutionary*

I have often wished I could spend a day with some master expositors I admire just to watch how they study and prepare to share the Word of God from the pulpit. How do they choose a text or strategize to help their people grasp the big picture? How would they decide how to balance preaching from both testaments or different genre of Scripture? What does the very personal thought process and the crafting of the sermon look like? And how do they show faithfulness to the text as the author has written it while acknowledging the entire canon and its testimony of Christ? That's why I love *Preach*! It affords the reader the opportunity to engage two great preachers in a warm conversation that will reap preaching dividends for a lifetime of ministry. Part philosophy, part methodology, but all encouragement, this is the best book on preaching I've read in a long time.

—Hershael W. York, associate dean, School of Theology
Victor & Louise Lester professor of Preaching at The Southern
Baptist Theological Seminary

This little book gets at the heart of expositional preaching in a clear, concise, and enjoyable way. The theological section is insightful and powerful, the Christ-centered emphasis is timely, and the practical instruction is helpful. The gracious, encouraging, and pastoral tone makes you want to improve but also allows you to marvel at the privilege of preaching. I loved hearing of the differences in approaches between Dever and Gilbert—from sermon introductions to sermon notes/manuscripts to "sermon walks." Both, driven by the same convictions, work at their craft in unique ways. I also love the various ways they do exposition, such as book overview sermons and preaching through large portions of Scripture. I plan on using this book in class for students preparing for ministry, but seasoned preachers will also find encouragement and help as they continue to preach the unsearchable riches of Christ.

—Tony Merida, lead pastor,
Imago Dei Church, Raleigh, North Carolina
and Associate Professor of Preaching
at Southeastern Baptist Theological Seminary

I've always considered it a privilege to spend time with Mark Dever—his fellowship has edified, encouraged, enlightened and enthused me. This book on preaching invites us into the ongoing conversation with his colleague Greg Gilbert. From their shared theological commitment to preaching God's Word, it provides a plethora of practical clues to the art of preaching a sermon. It will stimulate both the novice and the experienced to improve our preaching. Buy it for yourself or your pastor.

—Phillip Jenson
Dean of Sydney at St. Andrew's Cathedral, Sydney, Australia

preach

preach

[Theology Meets Practice]

Mark Dever Greg Gilbert

NASHVILLE, TENNESSEE

978-1-4336-7317-7

Published by B&H Publishing Group
Nashville, Tennessee

Dewey Decimal Classification: 251
Subject Heading: PREACHING \ SERMONS \ BIBLE

1 2 3 4 5 6 7 8 • 16 15 14 13 12

To all the men I have had the privilege
of teaching as CHBC Interns.
May God bless you as you proclaim His Word.

—Mark E. Dever

In Memory of Bro. D. C. "Bo" Mangum Jr.
Should God give me grace to preach so long and
so faithfully, I will be a blessed man indeed.

—Greg Gilbert

Contents

Acknowledgments

No book ever writes itself, and no author ever writes a book alone. We want to thank multiple people for their help and support in producing this book.

To Jonathan, Karen, Matt, Ryan, and all the others at 9Marks—your work, dear friends, is so good and useful for the church of Jesus Christ. We count it a privilege to work with you not just on this book but in the whole ministry of 9Marks. Thank you. May God give us many more years of work!

Thank you, too, to our good friends at B&H. For your partnership, your long-suffering, your patience, and your initiative, we're grateful. And we both look forward to a long and fruitful relationship.

To our churches, Capitol Hill Baptist and Third Avenue Baptist, we love you dearly. We love preaching to you, we love living in covenant with you, and we look forward to many more years of opening God's Word with you and growing together in maturity in Christ.

Finally, to our families. None of this, at all, would be possible without your encouragement and support. You give much more than you get in the writing of these books. We thank God for your partnership in the gospel, and we love you dearly.

Introduction

Not everybody in the world who sees a book called *Preach* decides to pick it up and read it. You have to be one of a pretty limited set of people to do that! Of course, that tells us—even two sentences into this book—that you must be one of those people.

There could be several different reasons why you decided to pick up this book. Maybe you're a church member who cares deeply about your pastor's work every Sunday in the pulpit, and you wanted to take a look at a book he might read. Maybe you're a Christian who's concerned about the preaching you hear every week in the church you attend. Maybe you're someone who isn't a Christian at all, but for whatever reason a book on the theology and practice of something as weird as preaching caught your attention. If any of those describe you, welcome! We're glad you picked this book up, and we hope it'll be beneficial to you as you flip through it.

By and large, though, we expect that most of the people who read this book are preachers—either men who have been preaching God's Word for a long time or those who haven't preached much at all, if ever. For that reason much of what we say in this book is going to be preaching "shop talk." In other words it's going to be highly practical, highly specific, and drawn from our own practices in preparation and delivery. Please take that into account as you read this book: we're not setting out to say that there's only *one way* to prepare for a sermon or to deliver it, *one way* to use introductions and conclusions, *one way* to think about illustrations, or *one way* to do most of the things we talk about in this book. Yes, sometimes we'll make a strong case for why we think one practice is better than others, but we trust you'll be able to take that advice and adapt it to your own situation and your own church.

Anytime you start writing a book, a moment always comes when you stop typing and the whole project nearly dies. It's the moment when these questions pop into your head: Why am *I* writing this book? What do *I* have to say about this that's worth anyone's reading? This book was no exception, and we can dispense with a few answers to that question immediately. For one, we're not writing this book because we in any way think we're the best preachers. Far from it! Both of us can name preachers—dozens of them—who are better preachers than we are. This is also not a mutual admiration society where each of us thinks the other guy is the best preacher out there. "No, no, *you're* the best." "No, *you* are!" In fact, believe it or not, Greg enjoys hearing other preachers more than he enjoys hearing Mark, and Mark enjoys plenty more than he enjoys Greg. So it's not that. We're also not writing this book because we have more experience at preaching than anyone else. Mark has more than fifteen years of experience as a senior pastor (nothing to scoff at, true, but not exactly the four, five, or six decades many other preachers have, either), and Greg's still thinking *five* years as a senior pastor sounds like forever.

So it's none of those reasons. I suppose the best answer to the question, Why are we writing this book? is that we have been blessed in God's providence to spend the better part of the last decade thinking and talking together about these issues. To be sure, the instructional traffic has been mostly one way (Mark teaching me, Greg), and 90 percent of what I know about preaching and *do* in preaching I have learned from Mark. But I trust it's not *all* been one way. Not *everything* I do is like Mark, and I think Mark may even have picked up two or three things (even four? Is that pushing it?) from things I've said to him.

When push comes to shove, the two of us have pretty different processes for preparing sermons. We think about application differently. We use different kinds of notes—Mark's are about thirteen pages for any given sermon; mine are about four. And while I'm sure anybody listening to my sermons will hear echoes of Mark in them, I think our *styles* of preaching are different. Among other things, I tend to walk around; Mark plants his feet behind the pulpit. We both use humor; Mark uses it better. I dress cooler. Mark uses lots of quotations; I don't. I tell more stories about myself and my kids than Mark does. Mark does extended, meaty introductions; mine are shorter and, frankly, cheaper.

Anyway, think of this book as a conversation between mentor and mentee, between a teacher and his longtime student who's just setting out on his maiden voyage. You'll see similarities, and you'll see differences. You'll see things we're sure of and other things we're not sure of at all but do anyway. But through it all, hopefully you'll also see a shared conviction that God's Word is the most powerful force in the universe. It gives life, it heals, it corrects, it changes lives. We're both convinced of that, and we hope that by reading this book you'll be convinced of it, too—whether that means the strengthening of a long-held conviction that's flagged in recent years or the birth of a new conviction you've never held before. And we hope that through that renewed conviction, you'll be spurred anew to preach God's Word with passion, accuracy, and boldness.

Before we press on, let us give you a few more specifics on why we thought a book like this might be useful to the church at this particular time. Three reasons come to mind.

First, we can see rising in the evangelical church a loss of confidence in the preached Word of God. Let's be honest—preaching is a strange thing to do. Our age is all about pithy sound bites and immediate interaction. Most of our communication is done by short editorials, shorter blog posts, even shorter updates on our Facebook pages, and most recently, 140-character Tweets. (Ever seen people try to have a theological discussion over Twitter? Heaven help us.) Our attention spans are trained and molded by television shows that switch camera angles every seven to eight seconds because we actually get bored if they wait any longer and by news programs that have to *argue* about the news because we're too bored and impatient just to be *told* about it. And then, in the middle of all that, we expect Christians to sit for thirty or forty minutes and *listen* to one guy talk. And they can't even Reply or Comment or +1 or Like what we're saying!

Probably in response to some of that and in an effort to meet people where their attention spans are, more than a few Christians have argued that the best way to move forward is for the church to adopt a kind of dialogical preaching where the Bible is taught not so much in the form of a sermon but in the form of a conversation—statements and questions and answers, more like a Sunday school class or small-group Bible study. In that way, the argument goes, people will stay more engaged with the teaching, they'll be able to interact with it, and they'll get their questions answered in a way that's just not possible when one person is preaching an extended, uninterrupted sermon.

Of course, we see clearly the point being made here, and in some ways it's a good one. In fact, both of us have opportunities in our churches where just that sort of teaching is done. But we also think significant things are lost when a congregation never hears the Word of God delivered at length, with power, in an uninterrupted sermon. Part of what we're trying to do in this book is show you what some of those things are and in the process increase your confidence in the power of God's Word *proclaimed* and not just *considered*.

Second, we see throughout much of the evangelical church a lack of confidence in biblical exposition. In recent years many evangelical Christians have argued persuasively for what is called "expositional preaching." Exposition is not a new development in the church. Some men have been doing it from their pulpits for decades, and we hope to show in this book that exposition is even the type of preaching the Bible itself presupposes. But in recent years more and more voices have been raised to advocate that preaching, in the main, be expositional in nature—that is, that it *expose* the Word of God to the listeners.

We're thankful for that renewed emphasis. But we've also noticed that more questions are being raised about expositional preaching: Where do we see it in the Bible? Doesn't exposition bore people out of their minds? Is it even possible to do exposition that isn't dry and lifeless? As a result of those questions, some evangelical preachers seem to be shying away from exposition. Sometimes they replace it with a steady diet of topical sermons, sometimes with character studies, sometimes even with things that strain the definition of preaching; but regardless of what replaces it, opening the Bible to a particular passage and preaching the meaning of that passage Sunday after Sunday is far from the normal practice in most evangelical churches.

We wish it were otherwise, though, and we will offer good, compelling answers to the objections people most often have against exposition. Part of what we're trying to do in this book is answer some of those objections and make a case—a biblical, theological, and practical case—for exposition.

Third, we want to work against the bad name that even some expositional preachers have given to expositional preaching. Let's be honest again—a lot of what flies under the name "expositional preaching" is just not good preaching. Some of the questions we asked above aren't entirely without merit, and they have plenty of empirical evidence backing them up. Both of us have sat under "expositional preaching" that wasn't much more than a running commentary on first-century Jewish backgrounds. We've heard preachers get lost in their texts and end their sermons with, "Well, we've run out of time. Wonderful how rich God's Word is, isn't it? We'll pick up here next week." We've heard others take simple passages and make them incomprehensibly complex. We've heard application to the heart that runs not much deeper than: "See? It says to love your neighbor. So . . . love your neighbors. Really love them. Love *on* them! Next point!" If expositional preaching has a bad name—and it does in some circles of evangelicalism—we who claim to preach expositionally can't entirely escape blame for it.

For that reason another thing we want to do in this book is put on paper some of the things we've learned through the years (or months, in Greg's case) about how to expose God's Word to a congregation in a way that's engaging, affecting, and convicting. Some of what we say is going to sound ridiculously small, even inconsequential. Other things might be entirely a matter of opinion. You're free to take or leave things as you find them helpful or not. But we hope you'll find at least a few things in these pages that will help you avoid a few mistakes both of us have made.

So that's it! Time for some shop talk about preaching. This book is made up of three different parts, each of which is trying to do something different. In Part One, we make a theological case for preaching the Word of God and then a specific case for expositional preaching in particular. We don't intend this to be a comprehensive systematic or biblical theology, so there will necessarily be some things we don't say. We simply want to show you from the Bible why we think preaching is so important and why we think the best way to do that is through exposition. In Part Two, we'll turn to some practical considerations about expositional preaching. How do you decide which text to preach from? What should be in an expositional sermon, and how do the parts fit together? How do you move from exegesis to theology to application? There are as many different ways to do most of those things as there are men who preach, but we hope hearing us talk about how we do it will be of some help or encouragement to you. And then there's Part Three. You'll read later in this book about how both of us try to solicit feedback on our sermons from certain people in our congregations. We thought it might be helpful, therefore, show you a little of what that looks like. Part Three, therefore, contains two transcripts of sermons—one from Greg and one from Mark—and scattered throughout those transcripts is a conversation we had with one another about those sermons. We give encouragement and criticism, we offer sugges-tions, we argue a little and make fun of each other, and we hope that all that together will show you something of what a "sermon review" would look like at both our churches.

Above all, we hope this book will be edifying to you no matter how experienced a preacher you are. If you're not experienced at all, we hope it'll be of some help to you in preparing to preach God's Word to His people. And if you *are* experienced as a preacher, then we hope it'll encourage you and maybe even give you some things to think about as you press on with the call God has given you. Regardless of how many times you've preached, though, we hope this book will reignite a passion in your heart for preaching the Bible. God's Word is our life, and it is the only hope of a dying world. What a privilege that it should be through our lips, our mouths, and our voices that the gospel of life should be proclaimed! May God bless the preaching of His Word.

[PART ONE]

Theology

CHAPTER ONE

God Speaks

———•◦•———

Ihaven't read many twenty-three-volume novels. In fact, I haven't read *any* twenty-three-volume novels. But if I did, I'd expect to find an author who had a lot to say. I'd expect insight or at least an ambition to insight. I'd expect character development and an exquisite plot, surprises, tragedies, and hilarity. In short, I'd expect to find *meaning* somewhere in the course of reading a twenty-three-volume novel.

If that's your assumption, too, then you've probably never read and enjoyed anything by Nigel Tomm. In 2008, Tomm managed to convince a publisher to print his twenty-three-volume novel, *The Blah Story*.[1] It's a work of magnificent ambition and sweeping aspiration—that aspiration being to write an 11.3-million-word story *without saying anything at all.* Don't believe it? Here's an excerpt from volume 16 of Tomm's work:

> As no one was blah any blah to blah, and no one blah
> needed blah, blah quietly blah blah away into the little blah
> where the blah were, and again blah a great blah of blah

when blah saw the blah, the little old blah pressed blah to blah something, and blah agreed; after blah a blah with blah and talking to the blah of their blah, blah, not blah to blah back to the blah, where it blah all so blah to blah, proceeded to blah through the blah, the blah were blah of blah blah blah, blah over the blah and blah not to blah a blah word of what blah being said blah with the blah were blah and blah smart blah, high blah in blah, and blah.

The publisher made a sporting attempt to get people to buy the books, touting them like this:

Overwhelmingly creative, Nigel Tomm demolishes the barrier of words and meaning, giving vitality and expressive strength to the pattern of his most exclusive novel— *The Blah Story*. It is a new way of conceiving text that frees the imagination, allowing you to personalize each and every word by your own creativity.

Allowing me to personalize each word . . . well, yes, that's one way to put it! Apparently the publisher's gamble didn't pay off too well, and readers weren't overly excited about having to write the whole story for themselves. All volumes are currently out of print!

God Speaks, and That Sets Him Apart

Nigel Tomm is not the only person to poke fun in recent decades at the idea of words and speech having meaning. In fact, entire worldviews claim that language—our communication with one another—is really not much more than a game and that each person invests whatever meaning he desires into the words he reads or hears. It's all a bunch of "blah blah blah," and we fill in the "blahs" with whatever best suits us, our needs, and our wants.

That's not how the Bible approaches words. Not even close.

From the first page of the Bible, words are enormously important to the God who made the universe. In fact, one of the most interesting themes of the Bible, as you read through it, is the argument it makes over and over again that it is precisely God's *words*—His power to speak, to command, to be heard and understood—that sets Him apart from the false gods His people are always tempted to worship. The God of the Bible is utterly unique, utterly singular, and utterly worthy of our worship; and one of the most important evidences for that is the fact that *God speaks*.

We Christians tend to take that fact for granted today. It's no big deal, really, for us to affirm that God speaks because we are so used to it. "Of course God speaks!" we say. "What kind of God would He be that couldn't speak?" So we read our Bibles, which we understand to be the *Word of God*; we read the stories of God speaking to Abraham, Isaac, Jacob, and Moses. We quote the prophets with their ringing cry, "Thus *says* the Lord," and we blithely affirm with John that Jesus was "the *Word* made flesh." And it all washes over us without ever our giving it a second thought.

It wasn't always that way. For the Israelites the fact that their God spoke to them—actually talked and communicated with them—wasn't so easy to take for granted. "Gods" were common in the Ancient Near East; every tribe and nation that surrounded Israel had their own gods and their own ways of worship, and all of them believed that their gods were real and that they acted. But one way those pagan gods never acted was in *speech*. They never talked. Only one God talked, and that was Yahweh, the God of Israel.

One of the most sarcastic, cutting passages in the entire Bible comes in the book of Isaiah where God unleashes a withering denunciation of the false gods His people have begun to worship. Instead of loving Him and trusting Him, the Israelites have turned to the idols of their pagan neighbors, and God makes a case over four chapters that they have made a monumentally foolish decision. Only He has the power to save them.

God's assault on the idols comes from a few different directions. He ridicules them first for being pieces of metal or wood or stone that had to be carved by craftsmen. Isaiah 41:7, for instance, has the amusing picture of one craftsman complimenting the work of another who has just made a god and then the even more hilarious image of the two of them working together to nail the god to the table so it doesn't topple over! In chapter 44, God invites His people to consider—in detail—exactly where their "gods" come from. First someone plants a tree, then he waits for the rain to nourish it, and eventually the tree is big enough to be cut down. "Then it becomes fuel for a man," God says (v. 15). "He takes part of it and warms himself; he kindles a fire and bakes bread." And then He comes to the punch line, its abruptness only adding to the ridiculousness of the scene: "Also he makes a god and worships it; he makes an idol and falls down before it."

You can almost hear the incredulity in God's voice there: "Seriously? You're going to cut down a tree, saw it in half, grill a steak over half of it, and then bow down and worship the other half?" The ridicule continues over the next couple of verses:

> Half of it he burns in the fire. Over the half he eats meat; he roasts it and is satisfied. Also he warms himself and says, "Aha, I am warm, I have seen the fire!" And the rest of it he makes into a god, his idol, and falls down to it and worships it. He prays to it and says, "Deliver me, for you are my god!" (vv. 16–17)

For all the obvious stupidity of it all, though, the worship of idols points to a deeper and sadder problem. Those who worship these false gods are not just ridiculous; they are blind and ignorant and dark hearted. Here's how God ends the passage, not so much with ridicule as with a lament for His people's deluded hearts:

> They know not, nor do they discern, for he has shut their eyes, so that they cannot see, and their hearts, so that they

cannot understand. No one considers, nor is there knowledge or discernment to say, "Half of it I burned in the fire; I
also baked bread on its coals; I roasted meat and have eaten.
And shall I make the rest of it an abomination? Shall I fall
down before a block of wood?" He feeds on ashes; a deluded
heart has led him astray, and he cannot deliver himself or
say, "Is there not a lie in my right hand?" (vv. 18–20)

All by itself the argument against the idols as being nothing but
"blocks of wood" was devastating. But there was more to be said.
It wasn't just that the idols had a humiliating origin; it was that
they couldn't *do* anything. More specifically—and here we come to
the most important point—the idols were unlike the God of Israel
precisely because they couldn't *speak*.

Look at how God addresses the idols in Isaiah 41:21–24. He calls
them, as a judge would call a defendant, to present proof of their reality,
evidence of their power. But notice specifically what He asks them to do:

> Set forth your case, says the LORD;
> bring your proofs, says the King of Jacob.
> Let them bring them, and tell us
> what is to happen.
> Tell us the former things, what they are,
> that we may consider them,
> that we may know their outcome;
> or declare to us the things to come.
> Tell us what is to come hereafter,
> that we may know that you are gods;
> do good, or do harm,
> that we may be dismayed and terrified.
> Behold, you are nothing,
> and your work is less than nothing;
> an abomination is he who chooses you.

God challenges the idols to speak. "Tell us!" He demands. Say something! Tell us what has happened in the past or what is to happen in the future. Do *something* so we can know that you're really gods and therefore worthy of our fear. But what does He get from them? Nothing. Just silence. So He hands down His judgment on them: "Behold, you are nothing, and your work is less than nothing."

The God of Israel, though, is the God who speaks, and that sets Him utterly apart from the idols:

> Thus says the LORD, the King of Israel
> and his Redeemer, the LORD of hosts:
>   "I am the first and I am the last;
> besides me there is no god.
>   Who is like me? Let him proclaim it.
> Let him declare and set it before me,
>   since I appointed an ancient people.
> Let them declare what is to come, and what will happen.
>   Fear not, nor be afraid;
> have I not told you from of old and declared it?
> And you are my witnesses!
>   Is there a God besides me?
> There is no Rock; I know not any." (Isa. 44:6–8)

There is no other god besides the God of Israel, and do you see what proves it? It is that He and He alone has spoken. He has told His people from old what is to come, and if anyone else would claim to be god, he too must *speak*.

The Primacy of God's Word

God's polemic against the idols in Isaiah 41–44 is not the only place in the Bible where God's *speaking* has priority. Over and over, the Bible's story holds out God's Word as that which sets Him apart and that to which human beings ought to give special attention.

In Genesis 1:1, God creates the heavens and the earth. And how does He do it? By speaking. In Genesis 2, He gives life to the lifeless body He's created from the dust. Again, how does He do it? By the breath of His mouth. When He reveals Himself to His people after rescuing them from slavery to Egypt, what does He give them? A picture of Himself? A terrifying *look* at His face? No, He gives them the Law; He *speaks* to His people and *tells* them who He is and who, therefore, they are to be.

Even in the way God commanded His people to design and build His temple, the primary way His people were to know Him was through His word, and that was utterly different from the pagan gods around them. Do you remember what was at the center of the temple, inside the holy of holies? In a typical pagan temple, at the center of the temple, in the most holy place where people came to worship, stood an image of the god. That's what people expected to see when they made their way into the presence of the god. They expected to *see* him. But that's not what the God of Israel told His people to put at the center of His temple. Instead, when a person walked into the holy of holies of Yahweh's temple, what he saw was not an image at all but rather a golden box. And inside that box were the tablets on which God had written the Ten Commandments. You see? The God of the Bible would be known by His people not primarily by *sight* but by *sound*. They would hear His Word, not see His face. They would know Him as the God who speaks.

The prophet Ezekiel learned this same lesson when he encountered the Lord on the banks of the Chebar canal in Babylon. The people of Israel had been carried off into exile, defeated in battle, and taken in chains across the desert to a land they had never known. It was a shocking turn of events. How could God allow His chosen people to be treated this way? How could He allow His holy city, Jerusalem, to be sacked and destroyed by the pagan Babylonians? The Bible doesn't say specifically, but you have to wonder if those were the kinds of questions Ezekiel was asking as he sat on the banks of the Chebar that day. If so, God answered him in a dramatic way—in a way, in fact, that still fascinates us and leads us to marvel and wonder at what Ezekiel must have seen that day.

Entire books have been written on the vision God gave to Ezekiel that day. Some scholars, trying to visualize for themselves what Ezekiel saw, have declared the whole thing to be nonsensical and Ezekiel himself to be clinically insane. One commentator went so far as to call him "a true psychotic, capable of great religious insight but exhibiting a series of diagnostic characteristics: catatonia, narcissistic-masochistic conflict, schizophrenic withdrawal, delusions of grandeur and of persecution. In short, he suffered from a paranoid condition common in many great spiritual leaders."[2]

But of course that misses the point entirely. Ezekiel wasn't a psychotic, and his visions weren't meant to be drawn or built. The "wheels within wheels" he saw weren't supposed to be taken as blueprints for construction. No, the vision Ezekiel saw was rich in symbolism, and it also—even in its resistance to being clearly pictured in our imaginations—communicates that God transcends us. He is greater than we are and more glorious than we could ever imagine.

We could say much about what Ezekiel saw, but one detail in particular stands out as peculiarly counter to the way we would probably have written the story. Do you remember the climax of Ezekiel's vision? After all the glorious images—the flashing storm, the creatures, the wheel, the eyes, the sapphire throne, the blazing figure of a man—do you remember what it all leads to? Here's how Ezekiel described it: "Such was the appearance of the likeness of the glory of the Lord. And when I saw it, I fell on my face, and I heard the voice of one speaking" (Ezek. 1:28).

The last phrase of that verse is stunning in its simplicity, isn't it? All the grandeur of the vision, all the glory of what Ezekiel saw led finally to this one, last, greatest thing: "I *heard* the voice of One *speaking*."

It's interesting how much weight the Bible puts on the words of God, isn't it? Most of us, when we imagine what an encounter with God might be like, tend to major on the visual. If we were guessing, without knowing in advance, what Ezekiel might have experienced in his encounter with God, our guess at how it all unfolded probably would have *started* with a voice and ended with a glorious, mind-blowingly beautiful vision. So it's interesting and challenging to us that the reality goes in exactly the opposite direction. First Ezekiel sees, and then he hears. And that *hearing* forms the basis of his relationship with God.

God's Speaking Is the Basis of our Relationship with Him

That simple truth is taught throughout the Bible. The fundamental basis of any person's relationship with God is that we hear His Word and respond to it. Think, for example, about Adam and Eve in the Garden of Eden. The striking thing about the intimacy of their relationship with God is not so much that they saw Him but that they heard Him and conversed with Him. He spoke to them, and they heard what He said and responded to it. When Satan moves to disrupt their relationship with God, he makes his attack directly on what they have heard from God: "Did God really say . . . ?" In the end Adam and Eve's rejection of God's Word defined their rebellion against Him because their hearing and obeying of His Word had defined their relationship with Him.

It was the same for Abraham. The beginning and foundation of his relationship with God was God's grace in speaking to him and calling him to leave his country and go to Canaan. The whole story of Israel begins with the words, "Now the Lord said to Abram" (Gen. 12). Think, too, of how God's covenant relationship with the newly redeemed, newly constituted nation of Israel began: it began with

God speaking His law to them. Thus Moses said to them after he had given them the Law:

> Take to heart all the words by which I am warning you today, that you may command them to your children, that they may be careful to do all the words of this law. For it is no empty word for you, but your very life. (Deut. 32:46–47)

If the people of Israel would enjoy a relationship with God, it would be through hearing, meditating on, remembering, and obeying His Word. The prophet Samuel's relationship with God, too, began by hearing His voice. First Samuel 3:7 is interesting: "Now Samuel did not yet know the LORD, and the word of the LORD had not yet been revealed to him." Do you see how "knowing the Lord" and "hearing the word of the Lord" are brought together here? Despite all his time serving in the temple, Samuel did not truly know the Lord until His Word was revealed to him.

Of course, all this comes to its pinnacle in Jesus Christ, the incarnate Word of God. You see, it is in Jesus that God is most fully and most perfectly revealed. It is in Him that we come to know God and that our relationship with God is established. The apostle John writes about this in the first chapter of his Gospel. "The Word became flesh," he says, "and dwelt among us, and we have seen his glory, glory as of the only Son from the Father, full of grace and truth. . . . No one has ever seen God; the only God, who is at the Father's side, he has made him known" (John 1:14, 18). John's language is dense and packed with meaning, but the essential point is clear. If we as sinful human beings would know God the Father, it will only be through the Son who knows Him perfectly, who is at His side, and who makes Him known to us. As the author of the book of Hebrews says: "Long ago, at many times and in many ways, God spoke to our fathers by the prophets, but in these last days he has spoken to us by his Son" (Heb. 1:1).

God Speaks, and Therefore We Preach

As preachers of God's Word, we should understand how important and amazing it is that our God is a speaking God. He didn't have to speak, at least not to us. When Adam and Eve sinned against Him in the Garden, He could have let His last words to them—for all eternity—be the curse He pronounced against them. "You are dust, and to dust you shall return," He could have said (Gen. 3:19). And then silence. God could have left us in darkness and ignorance to live out our days as rebels and to die under His wrath, without ever knowing Him. Understanding that, it is a mark of the most amazing mercy and love that God continued to care for human beings after we rebelled against Him, that He continued to speak to us and to reveal Himself to us, especially in the person of His Son, Jesus.

All this helps us understand some of the poignant symbolism at work when one man stands before a congregation to proclaim God's Word. Some church leaders recently have argued for a modification of our idea of preaching. For one person to address a host of others in a long monologue, they argue, is simply wrong. It is tyrannizing, depersonalizing, and dehumanizing, a vestige of the Enlightenment or of Hellenistic thinking that we have long since gotten past.

We think that's wrong. In fact, we think the sermon as monologue—one person speaking while others listen—is both an accurate and a powerful symbol of our spiritual state and God's grace. For one person to speak God's Word while others listen is a depiction of God's gracious self-disclosure and of our salvation being a gift. Anytime God speaks in love to human beings it is an act of grace. We do not deserve it, and we contribute nothing to it. The act of preaching is a powerful symbol of that reality.

The picture of the first recorded sermon in the book of Acts is an arresting illustration of this. It was not a humanly planned meeting that brought these people together. God had poured out His Spirit, according to His own purposes, and then it fell to Peter to address the crowd and explain what was happening. He quoted God's Word to them from Psalm 16, Psalm 110, and the prophet Joel, and then he spoke to them. He told them what this meant and how it was relevant to them. Even their question, "What shall we do?" (Acts 2:37) points to their ignorance and need to hear. Peter preached to them a message they would not otherwise have known. It wasn't a dialogue or a discussion. It was a heralding of news previously unknown. Peter himself had not understood Jesus' identity apart from the divine and supernatural light God Himself had given him, and the people in Jerusalem would not understand it either unless God revealed it to them.

This is always the way it is with Christian preaching. The empty pulpit in many of our church buildings well displays the spiritual reality. We run around seeking life for our churches and life for ourselves through a million different methods, and the one means God has given for bringing people into a relationship with Himself stands neglected and disdained. In the act of preaching—a congregation hearing the voice of one man who stands behind the Scriptures—God has given us an important symbol of the fact that we come into relationship with Him by His Word. Just as surely as Abram was called to God by the word of promise addressing him, so we as Christians are made God's people by believing God and trusting His promises. In a word, we come into relationship with God through faith, and "faith comes," Paul tells us in Romans 10, "from *hearing*, and hearing through the word of Christ."

There is only one God, and He is a relational and communicating, personal being who speaks to us and initiates relationship with us. Those powerful, life-giving truths are not only proclaimed but also powerfully symbolized by the preaching of God's Word. He speaks, and therefore we preach.

[CHAPTER TWO]

The Power of God's Word

———— ◆ ————

Words have power. We all say it, and we all know it to be true. Words can heal or hurt, break down or build up. They can create, destroy, or even change reality. My favorite part of performing a wedding ceremony is when I stand before the bride and groom and say something like, "Now in the sight of God and these witnesses, I declare that you are husband and wife, in the name of the Father, the Son, and the Holy Spirit." Those words have power, don't they? They effectively change the relationship of that man and woman standing before me. Before I say them, they aren't married. But after I say them, everything changes; they're husband and wife, with all the benefits, privileges, and responsibilities that come along with that.

So it's certainly true to say that our words have power. But even so, it's another thing entirely to say that *God's* Word has power. Our words may wound or encourage, even sometimes create new relationships and statuses that weren't there before; but they can't do what God's words can do. They can't still storms or make something out of nothing. And perhaps above all, our words cannot—and never will have the power—to give life to those who are dead. Only God's Word can do that.

God Creates and Gives Life by His Word

The Bible begins, in its very first sentences, by teaching us about the power of God's Word. Into a world of darkness and void—that is, into a world of nothingness—God speaks and brings into being everything that exists in the universe. If you stop and think about it, that is an awesome display of power. It would have been amazing in itself for God to create the world out of *something*, to have fashioned it from unformed, shapeless matter into something of order and beauty. But He didn't do that. Instead, He simply spoke. "Let there be light," and there was light. "Let there be fish," and there were fish. "Let there be birds," and there were birds! As the author of Hebrews says, "We understand that the universe was created by the word of God, so that what is seen was not made out of things that are visible" (Heb. 11:3). Read the first chapter of Genesis, and the overwhelming impression you're left with is that God's Word has tremendous power—even power to create *ex nihilo*.

That impression only strengthens as the story unfolds, for it quickly becomes clear that the word of God's mouth not only calls into existence things that were not, but it also has the power to give life where there was no life. Think for instance about God's creating Adam. Yes, God fashions Adam from the dirt of the ground, a point that will become important later in showing just how dependent on God for life Adam really is. But what gives Adam life, animates and transforms him from a lump of clay into a moving, breathing, living, loving *person*? Genesis 2:7 tells the story like this: "Then the LORD God formed the man of dust from the ground and breathed into his nostrils the breath of life, and the man became a living creature." Life came to Adam from the breath of God's mouth.

Not surprisingly, "God's breath" is often in Scripture linked powerfully with His Word. In Psalm 33:6, for example, the psalmist says: "By the word of the LORD the heavens were made, and by the breath of his mouth all their host." Hebrew poetry is marked by the frequent use of "parallelism," in which a poet will repeat an idea with two different sets of words. That obviously has enormous devotional promise; it forces us to slow down in our reading and think a little more deeply about what the poet is saying. Parallelism can also be useful, though, in helping us to understand more precisely what a specific phrase or word means as the poet uses it. Here, the "word of the Lord" and "the breath of his mouth" are put in parallel as the means by which the Lord made the heavens and their host. God's "Word" and His "breath" are the same.

You can see this connection of God's breath and His Word again in Isaiah's prophecy of the coming Messiah in Isaiah 11. There the prophet foretells the coming of a "branch" from the "root of Jesse" who will judge the earth in righteousness. He will "judge the poor" and "decide with equity for the meek" (v. 4). All this the prophet describes as the Messiah "strik[ing] the earth with the rod of his mouth." In other words, the judgments that fall on the unjust inhabitants of the earth will be like the punishing strokes of a discipline rod. But look at the phrase that comes immediately after that: "And with the breath of his lips he shall kill the wicked." It's not that He'll literally "blow them away"; this is metaphorical language, after all. The text is saying that by His judgments against them, the Messiah will condemn the wicked and destroy them. Again, the breath of His mouth is equated with His Word.

The apostle Paul uses the same kind of language in 2 Thessalonians 2:8, when he says that Jesus, when He returns, will kill the lawless one "with the breath of his mouth." And look at how the book of Revelation describes that day of final judgment and how the returning King Jesus destroys those arrayed against Him:

> Then I saw heaven opened, and behold, a white horse! The one sitting on it is called Faithful and True, and in righteousness he judges and makes war. . . . From his mouth comes a sharp sword with which to strike down the nations, and he will rule them with a rod of iron. . . . And I saw the beast and the kings of the earth with their armies gathered to make war against him who was sitting on the horse and against his army. And the beast was captured, and with it the false prophet who in its presence had done the signs by which he deceived those who had received the mark of the beast and those who worshiped its image. These two were thrown alive into the lake of fire that burns with sulfur. And the rest were slain by the sword that came from the mouth of him who was sitting on the horse, and all the birds were gorged with their flesh. (Rev. 19:11, 15, 19–21)

Jesus "strikes down the nations" and slays those arrayed against Him by means of "a sharp sword that came from his mouth." What a strange picture! I have seen pictures—well meaning, I'm sure—of a majestic King Jesus riding out of the East on a magnificent white horse with a gold crown on His head . . . and holding a sword between His teeth. I have no doubt that's what John saw in his vision, but the point isn't that we should expect to see Jesus literally holding His sword between His teeth when He returns and then shaking His head furiously back and forth to slay His foes! No, this is apocalyptic imagery, and strange details like this *mean* something. They point us to something else. In this case the sword that comes from Jesus' mouth symbolizes His Word. Just as Isaiah prophesied, He will strike down the nations by His *judgments* against them, by His breath, by His Word.

Do you see the significance of all this? When God "blows the breath of life" into Adam's nostrils, we're to understand that act to be a continuation of His creation of the world *by the power of His Word*. God's Word brings into existence things that are not, and it gives life where there was no life. Jesus' own ministry brings this point to a brilliant head. Over and over again, He proves that His Word—God's Word—has the power to heal and to give life. In Matthew 8, for example, it is His bare word—"Go; let it be done" (v. 13)—that heals the centurion's servant. In Mark 5, it is the power of His Word—"Little girl, I say to you, arise!" (v. 41)—that brings the synagogue ruler's daughter back to life. In John 11, it is His word— "Lazarus, come out" (v. 43)—breaks death's grip on His friend and calls the *formerly* dead man out of his tomb.

Life to Dry Bones

Perhaps the most dramatic example of this in the Old Testament comes in Ezekiel's vision of the dry bones in Ezekiel 37. It's a magnificent story not just because it reaffirms that God's Word gives life but because it pushes our understanding of that truth from the merely physical to the spiritual. See, the vision of the dry bones coming to life isn't teaching finally that God can give physical life to physical bones; we already knew that. We've known it since the sixth day of creation. No, the vision of the dry bones is teaching us that God's Word also gives *spiritual* life to the *spiritually* dead. Here's what Ezekiel writes:

> The hand of the LORD was upon me, and he brought me
> out in the Spirit of the LORD and set me down in the
> middle of the valley; it was full of bones. And he led me
> around among them, and behold, there were very many on

the surface of the valley, and behold, they were very dry.
(Ezek. 37:1–2)

Not just dry but *very* dry. And not just many bones but *very* many bones. The vision God gives Ezekiel here is of a vast army that has been utterly and catastrophically defeated. There were no survivors, not even one left to bury the remains of his dead comrades. This is a picture of utter and total defeat, death, and lifelessness. It's a scene of complete despair.

And then God speaks, not to give life to the bones but to question Ezekiel. "Son of man," He says, "can these bones live?" (v. 3). What a question! I imagine that if Ezekiel had been with one of his friends (did he have any?), he would have turned and said, "You have to be kidding." But he knows to whom he is speaking, and so he answers with humility and admirable faith: "O Lord GOD, you know." What comes next is astonishing in both its simplicity and its apparent foolishness. God tells Ezekiel to preach!

> Then he said to me, "Prophesy over these bones, and say to them, O dry bones, hear the word of the LORD. Thus says the Lord GOD to these bones: Behold, I will cause breath to enter you, and you shall live. And I will lay sinews upon you, and will cause flesh to come upon you, and cover you with skin, and put breath in you, and you shall live, and you shall know that I am the LORD." (Ezek. 37:4–6)

Did you catch the really jarring statement at the beginning of that passage? "O dry bones, hear the word of the LORD!" Ezekiel is supposed to stand on the edge of that valley and call on the dry bones to *hear*! It's insane. And, yet again, Ezekiel knows who is commanding him to do this, and so he does it. And guess what?

> So I prophesied as I was commanded. And as I prophesied, there was a sound, and behold, a rattling, and the bones

came together, bone to its bone. And I looked, and behold, there were sinews on them, and flesh had come upon them, and skin had covered them. But there was no breath in them. Then he said to me, "Prophesy to the breath; prophesy, son of man, and say to the breath, Thus says the Lord GOD: Come from the four winds, O breath, and breathe on these slain, that they may live." So I prophesied as he commanded me, and the breath came into them, and they lived and stood on their feet, an exceedingly great army. (Ezek. 37:7–10)

That must be one of the most dramatic passages in all the Bible. The rattling, the movement of the bones together to form bodies, the sinews and flesh and skin stretching around them—it's all so vivid. But don't miss the point! Here's how the Lord explains to Ezekiel what he has just experienced:

Then he said to me, "Son of man, these bones are the whole house of Israel. Behold, they say, 'Our bones are dried up, and our hope is lost; we are indeed cut off.' Therefore prophesy, and say to them, Thus says the Lord GOD: Behold, I will open your graves and raise you from your graves, O my people. And I will bring you into the land of Israel. And you shall know that I am the LORD, when I open your graves, and raise you from your graves, O my people. And I will put my Spirit within you, and you shall live, and I will place you in your own land. Then you shall know that I am the LORD; I have spoken, and I will do it, declares the LORD." (Ezek. 37:11–14)

God is not giving Ezekiel an anatomy lesson or even a reiteration of His power to give physical life. He's teaching the prophet about the condition of the human soul in its sin and His power—by His Word—to give it *spiritual* life. The nation of Israel, exiled to Babylon, displaced from the Promised Land, disobedient and disgraced, is little more than a pile of desiccated bones. And yet God will make them live again. He will open their graves, put His Spirit in them, and they will live again.

I wonder if Ezekiel ever lost his confidence that God's Word was powerful to bring spiritual life to His people. If so, we have to hope that his mind wandered back to this vision of the valley of the dry bones and that his faith in God's Word was renewed by the memory. The Bible unfolds an amazing truth for us: when God creates and gives life, He does so through His Word.

The Power and Authority of God's Word Preached

Now if that's the case, it stands to reason that we as Christians—and especially we as church leaders—would take care to make the proclamation of God's Word the central component of our ministry. When competing priorities and competing philosophies tempt us sorely to displace the preaching of the Word from the center, the valley of the dry bones—not to mention the life given to Adam, the destruction of evil by "God's breath," the raising of Lazarus, and all the rest—ought to remind us that true spiritual-life-giving power is found in God's Word. That is how our God, in His wisdom, has determined to give life to His people.

We wonder if part of the loss of confidence in God's Word preached is due, ultimately, to a theological misunderstanding of exactly what preaching is in the first place. Think of it like this: if preaching is simply a way—one way among many—of ascertaining new knowledge about God and the Bible, then there are myriad ways for a person to do that. Reading books, watching videos, listening to podcasts, and having conversations with other Christians all fill that bill. Similarly, if preaching is nothing more than one man doing a bit of public meditation on spiritual truths, then there are countless ways for people to get that benefit. Why not meditate on God's truth together, in a conversation, for instance?

But if preaching really is the proclamation of God's life-giving, *ex nihilo* creating Word, then the stakes are raised considerably, and it's no longer a matter of preference whether we do it or not. It's literally a matter of life and death. The Bible presents the act of preaching as having just that sort of power and authority. It is the preached Word, it seems, which the Holy Spirit uses in a unique way to give life and ignite faith in a person's soul. Look for example at what Paul says in 1 Thessalonians 1:2–5. The gospel he proclaimed to them came "not only in word," he says, but also "in power and in the Holy Spirit." What Paul proclaimed to the Thessalonians was, yes, words. But it was more than words; it was words clothed in power and ignited by the Holy Spirit to bring spiritual life where there had been none before. And what was the result? That the Thessalonians' faith "sounded forth" (v. 8) all over the region and indeed went forth "everywhere!" There was power in the preached word.

Another passage instructive in this regard comes in Matthew 10 at the end of Jesus' discourse to His twelve apostles, whom He is about to send out to proclaim His kingship over Israel. Until that point in the book, Jesus has been making that case Himself, and His disciples have been watching, learning, and being prepared. In 10:1, though, Jesus calls to Himself twelve of His followers and gives them authority "over unclean spirits, to cast them out, and to heal every disease and every affliction" (Matt. 10:1). Moreover, He charges them to preach the message of the kingdom—that is, Jesus's kingship— which is precisely the message Jesus Himself has been preaching. Do you see what He's doing? Jesus is giving these twelve men authority and responsibility to do exactly what He Himself has been doing and then sending them out to do that work. It's interesting to notice in the first two verses of Matthew 10 that the twelve start out being called "disciples," but after they are given authority from Jesus, they are called "apostles" or "sent ones." The distinction doesn't hold perfectly; the twelve are still followers of Jesus even as they go on their mission. But it is still instructive to note that they don't commission *themselves* as "sent ones." They're only given that appellation after Jesus *sends* them.

What's interesting to see about the instructions Jesus gives them in the rest of the chapter, at least for our purposes, is the way authority resides so powerfully in the words they will proclaim. Take verses 14–15, for instance. Jesus tells His apostles that if any house or town will not listen to their words, they are to shake the dust off their feet against it. Now shaking the dust off one's feet was a dramatic insult coming from a Jewish person; it was the expression of a heartfelt conviction that God was going to judge that house or town and that the judgment would be so bad that a God-fearing Jew wouldn't even want the *dirt* of that town anywhere near him when it fell. Jesus' words confirm that: "Truly, I say to you, it will be more bearable on the day of judgment for the land of Sodom and Gomorrah than for that town." That is a terrifying promise, but the important thing to see is how tightly the judgment is tied to the apostle's message. To receive their word is to receive God's Word and all the blessings that entails. To reject their word is to reject God's Word, and to bring on oneself all the horrors of judgment.

The same point is made again at the end of the discourse, in Matthew 10:40. Here's what Jesus tells His apostles in conclusion: "Whoever receives you receives me, and whoever receives me receives him who sent me." That's an extraordinary statement of the authority that inheres in the apostles' preaching. Do you see what Jesus is saying? Being in relationship with God is finally about receiving—that is, believing, accepting as true, relying on—the gospel preached from human lips. Follow the logic backward: the one who receives "the one who sent [Jesus]" is precisely the one who receives Jesus. And who receives Jesus? The one who receives "you," that is, the preachers. That doesn't mean simply being nice to them as people. The prior part of the chapter makes it clear that what's in view here is receiving them in the sense of receiving *their message*. Amazing: the means of receiving God, of knowing Him and being known by Him, resides in the proclamation of the word—in preaching.

In 2 Corinthians 5, Paul writes this wonderful passage about his preaching ministry: "Therefore we are ambassadors for Christ, God making his appeal through us. We implore you on behalf of Christ, be reconciled to God" (v. 20). Paul here seems to draw on the same logic Jesus taught in Matthew 10. When Paul preaches, he says, it is not just words from his lips; it is "God *making his appeal through us!*" Thus for a person to hear and receive Paul's preaching of the gospel is for that person to receive none other than *God's* appeal through Paul to be reconciled to Him through Jesus.

Do you think of your own preaching of God's Word in these ways? Do you think of it as an authoritative heralding of God's own appeal for reconciliation? Do you realize that it is by receiving your proclamation of the Scriptures that people receive Jesus and therefore receive God? You should. Preaching is not finally a matter of giving a few thoughts here and there *about* God or the Bible. It is the proclamation of an authoritative message from the throne room of heaven itself: *Be reconciled to God through Jesus!* Understanding that theological truth about preaching can make all the difference between a milque-toast preaching ministry that just makes suggestions about a few things "we might want to think about" and a preaching ministry that heralds the good news, direct from the throne of God, that those who trust Jesus and confess Him as Lord will find mercy, forgiveness, salvation—and new life!—in His hand.

[CHAPTER THREE]

The Centrality of
Expositional Preaching

———————

Theology affects practice. We all know that's true. The ideas we hold in our minds, the things we take to be *true*, always affect the way we act and live. The way we think about the family, for example, affects how we live in our own families. The way we think about our jobs affects how we act as we do those jobs. How we understand the nature and significance of the church affects how we act as church members and church leaders. And what we understand to be true about preaching affects how we preach and how much priority we give to preaching in our local churches.

If what we've said in the last couple of chapters is true—that God's Word gives life and preaching is the proclamation of God's Word—then a couple of things become inescapable in our thinking about and practice of preaching.

Preaching Must Expose God's Word to God's People

First, the nature of preaching as the heralding of God's Word means that any and all Christian preaching necessarily derives its authority from being rooted in and tethered tightly to God's Word, the Scriptures. Put more sharply, anything that is *not* rooted in and tethered tightly to God's Word is not preaching at all. It's just a speech. We don't have space here to make the entire case for the Bible being God's Word. Most people reading this book, we trust, already believe that, and others have made that case ably and effectively. Suffice it to say the Bible makes that claim for itself, Jesus Himself made it of the Old Testament, and the apostles made it of the writings of the New Testament. The Bible is the Word of God written, and therefore any preaching that truly heralds God's Word must take its message, from start to finish, from the Bible.

Given that, we believe the kind of preaching that tends most to the health of the church and the maturity of believers is *expositional preaching.* Now that's a hot term in the church these days, and like other hot terms it has probably been defined in more ways than are actually helpful. Most essentially, the term just has to do with preaching that *exposes* God's Word to God's people, that opens it up to them and applies it to their hearts so that they may understand it and obey it. To put it in a little more detail, here's a working definition of expositional preaching. *Expositional preaching is preaching in which the main point of the biblical text being considered becomes the main point of the sermon being preached.* In other words, if Paul was trying to get a certain point across in Ephesians 3, an expositional sermon on Ephesians 3 will take as its own main point not an implication of Ephesians 3, not a secondary or tertiary point of Ephesians 3, not a meditation on some ramifications of Ephesians 3, but precisely the main point Paul was trying to get across in Ephesians 3. It will *expose* Ephesians 3—its meaning, its point, its heart, its thrust, its passion—to the congregation. And of course, in the process (and perhaps more importantly), it will expose the congregation to Ephesians 3.

Now there are several things we should say up front in order to avoid confusion, especially about what we are *not* saying in this definition of expositional preaching. Here are a few:

1. We're not saying expositional preaching has to go verse by verse through a book of the Bible. You may think that's the case, and as this book progresses, we're going to argue for the wisdom of something similar to that approach. But we think it's entirely possible to preach a series on prayer, each sermon of which is an expositional sermon on a different passage of Scripture's teaching about prayer. The important thing is not that the texts be sequential; it's that each text be allowed to speak, through the sermon, its own main message in its own context.[3]

2. We're not saying expositional preaching rules out topical preaching as a legitimate practice. Sometimes topical sermons are a great way to give a church a comprehensive look at what the Bible says about a particular topic. Of course, that means sometimes you'll be making a second- or third-level point of a particular text the main point. That's perfectly fine, of course, but it will help a congregation learn to study and understand their Bibles if you acknowledge that's what you're doing. You don't want your congregation to think that the main point of Luke 2:10–14 is that *angels actually do sing!*—even if they do need to know that eventually. We're going to argue in this book that the best long-term diet for a church is a preaching ministry that makes its way through books; God didn't inspire the Bible topically, and there must be a reason for that. More on that later. But we're not saying that topical sermons are illegitimate or wrong or not helpful to a church.

3. We're not saying expositional preaching is just a series of lectures, the main goal of which is information transfer. That's one of the raps we frequently hear against expositional preaching—that it is a boring, irrelevant, unapplied lecture on a text of Scripture. You get first-century Jewish backgrounds, long discourses on Greek prepositions,

Hebrew syntax, and what "therefores are there for"; and you walk away with your mind full and your heart unbothered. That's emphatically *not* what we have in mind when we encourage expositional preaching. To expose a text of Scripture to a congregation means that you expose it to their hearts and their hearts to it. You explain to your congregation the thrust of the text—which seldom, by the way, requires any explanation at all of the aorist aspect—and then you follow the thrust of that text all the way to the heart in application.

4. We're not saying expositional preaching is marked by any particular style. It's not necessarily professorial or charismatic or young or old or stodgy or exciting or Deverian or Gilbertian. Expositional preaching is a method, not a style. Some preachers will have a professorial, learned demeanor as they unfold a text; others will be hilarious. Mark preaches to a large number of Congressional staffers; Greg preaches to a large number of college students. There are differences in style even between us and even larger differences of style between us and other expositional preachers. Style isn't the point; method is.

5. We're not saying expositional preaching is not evangelistic preaching. It is, and it must be! Jesus taught His disciples that every text in the Bible points ultimately to Him. So should our sermons. If we're preaching the Bible, and we're rightly discerning its meaning, then every sermon, one way or another, will make its way to Jesus and His identity as Lord and Savior. An expositional sermon that has not made its way to Jesus has not understood its text rightly.[4]

So those are some things we don't mean by expositional preaching. What we mean, to say it again, is *preaching in which the main point of the biblical text being considered becomes the main point of the sermon being preached.*

But Where's That in the Bible?

Of course, one of the first issues we have to consider is whether this kind of preaching shows up in the Bible. And we have to admit, right up front, that we don't see much of anything in the pages of Scripture that looks precisely like our sermon notes. But don't close the book! It's not as simple as all that.

The fact is, the Bible has lots of different kinds of preaching. You have Jeremiah's jeremiads, Jesus' parables, Moses' exposition of the law, Paul's logical reasoning, Ezekiel's . . . well, you have Ezekiel, don't you? And the main thing to see in all those kinds of preaching is that all the preachers are about the work of proclaiming God's Word to their listeners. That's what they understood they were doing, and in fact *not* to do that as a prophet or preacher was to default in your responsibility and call condemnation upon yourself. So Jeremiah says to those who would presume to prophesy (or preach!) what God has not said:

> And the LORD said to me: "The prophets are prophesying lies in my name. I did not send them, nor did I command them or speak to them. They are prophesying to you a lying vision, worthless divination, and the deceit of their own minds. Therefore thus says the LORD concerning the prophets who prophesy in my name although I did not send them, and who say, 'Sword and famine shall not come upon this land': By sword and famine those prophets shall be consumed." (Jer. 14:14–15)

Those who would presume to speak for God do well to make sure that what they say is what He says. Exposing God's Word is the aim of every prophet and preacher of God in the Bible.

We should recognize, too, the difference between Old Testament prophets, the apostles, and us. That helps to explain in a big way why we don't see those people preaching in exactly the same way we're advocating here—the reading, explanation, and application of a particular text of Scripture. The difference is simple but profound: the Word of God came directly to the prophets and apostles. It does not come directly to us; we know it through the Bible. They wrote Scripture; we read it.

That's also true, in an even more profound way, for Jesus. He *was* God, and therefore He proclaimed God's Word in an utterly unique way. Occasionally we hear people say that they don't preach expositionally because they want to preach like Jesus. What they mean by that, visually, is that they want to take a spiritual truth, come up with an illuminating story about it, and then tell that story. That's a nice sentiment, but we think preachers who say that sort of thing aren't thinking far enough. They're not giving Jesus enough credit. The fact is, most Christian preachers (who believe the Bible is the Word of God, anyway) wouldn't *dream* of preaching like Jesus preached. Not *really*. There's no way they'd stand in front of their congregations and say, "You have read in the Bible that . . . but *I* say to you . . . !" That kind of authority was Jesus' and Jesus' alone. He is the fulfillment of the Law and the Prophets. We are not. He is the Son of God. We are not. Every word that dropped from His lips was the Word of God. We speak the Word of God only insofar as we preach what the Bible says.

Actually, that is exactly what we see the non-prophet, non-apostle, non-Son-of-God preachers doing throughout the Bible; they preach the Scriptures, explaining them and applying them to their listeners. Think for example of the levitical priests. In addition to offering sacrifices in the temple worship, they were also charged with teaching the Law to the people of Israel, instructing them in it and exhorting them to obey it. Deuteronomy 33:10 explains their basic job description: "They shall teach Jacob your rules and Israel your law; they shall put incense before you and whole burnt offerings on your altar." Ezra the scribe understood the same thing about his charge. When the people of Israel returned to Jerusalem from their exile in Babylon, this is what happened:

> And all the people gathered as one man into the square
> before the Water Gate. And they told Ezra the scribe to
> bring the Book of the Law of Moses that the LORD had
> commanded Israel. So Ezra the priest brought the Law

before the assembly, both men and women and all who could understand what they heard, on the first day of the seventh month. And he read from it facing the square before the Water Gate from early morning until midday, in the presence of the men and the women and those who could understand. And the ears of all the people were attentive to the Book of the Law. And Ezra the scribe stood on a wooden platform that they had made for the pur-pose. . . . And Ezra opened the book in the sight of all the people, for he was above all the people, and as he opened it all the people stood. And Ezra blessed the LORD, the great God, and all the people answered, "Amen, Amen," lifting up their hands. And they bowed their heads and worshiped the LORD with their faces to the ground. Also Jeshua, Bani, Sherebiah, Jamin, Akkub, Shabbethai, Hodiah, Maaseiah, Kelita, Azariah, Jozabad, Hanan, Pelaiah, the Levites, helped the people to understand the Law, while the people remained in their places. They read from the book, from the Law of God, clearly, and they gave the sense, so that the people understood the reading. (Neh. 8:1–8)

The sense of drama in this passage is palpable. It's like a basket-ball highlight reel that shows the ball slamming into the hoop over and over again. "And Ezra brought the book of the Law . . . so he brought the book of the Law . . . and he read from it . . . and he stood on a wooden platform . . . and he opened the book . . . and he opened it . . . and he read from the book . . . so the people understood the reading!" Swish! Ezra wasn't acting as a prophet here. The word of God wasn't coming to him directly. He knew, though, that what the people needed, more desperately than anything else, was to hear the Word of God. So what did he do? He read and explained the Bible.

As if that weren't enough, it turns out that expositional proc-lamation happens a whole lot more often in the Bible than we may think—even by the apostles and Jesus himself! Luke 24 recounts what can only be described as a massive expositional sermon preached on the entire Old Testament by Jesus Himself:

> And he said to them, "O foolish ones, and slow of heart to believe all that the prophets have spoken! Was it not necessary that the Christ should suffer these things and enter into his glory?" And beginning with Moses and all the Prophets, he interpreted to them in all the Scriptures the things concerning himself. (vv. 25–27)

Granted, it was a sermon preached to two people but Jesus was explaining the Scriptures to those two people. "Beginning with Moses and all the Prophets, he interpreted to them *in all the Scriptures* the things concerning himself."

Now presumably he did that so that those two disciples could do it for others. And that's exactly what we see happening as the word of God begins to advance. In Acts 2, on the day of Pentecost, Peter stands and preaches a sermon in which he expounds portions of Joel 2, Psalm 16, and Psalm 110 in order to explain to the people what has just happened and its basis in the death and resurrection of Jesus. No, it doesn't look like mine, but that's an expositional sermon! It exposes the meaning of biblical texts and exhorts the listeners to act on them. In Acts 7, also, Stephen's sermon to the Sanhedrin is a long exposition of the story of the Old Testament. He unfolds that story and explains how it finds its fulfillment in Jesus. Again, it doesn't look precisely like mine, but Stephen's is an expositional sermon. The book of Hebrews, too, seems to be an expositional sermon in its own right. Several features of the book make it look like it was meant to be delivered verbally, and the whole structure of it is a series of explanations and applications of particular Old Testament texts. Chapter 1, for example, expounds Psalm 110. Chapter 2 expounds Psalm 8. Chapters 3 and 4 expound parts of Psalm 95. Chapter 5 expounds Psalm 2 and Psalm 110. Chapter 7 expounds Genesis 14 and Psalm 110. Chapter 8 expounds Jeremiah 31. And on and on and on. Again, it doesn't look like mine, but Hebrews is an expositional sermon. Whoever preached it, read and explained the Bible.

These aren't just one-offs, either. They seem to be examples of the general pattern of apostolic preaching. Consider these verses that describe Paul's way of proclaiming Jesus among the Jews:

In Ephesus:

> And he entered the synagogue and for three months spoke boldly, reasoning and persuading them about the kingdom of God. (Acts 19:8)

In Damascus:

> But Saul increased all the more in strength, and confounded the Jews who lived in Damascus by proving that Jesus was the Christ. (Acts 9:22)

In Athens:

> So he reasoned in the synagogue with the Jews and the devout persons. (Acts 17:17)

In Corinth:

> And he reasoned in the synagogue every Sabbath, and tried to persuade Jews and Greeks. (Acts 18:4)

So Paul reasoned and persuaded and confounded. He worked to "prove that Jesus was the Christ." But how? How do you persuade someone that Jesus is the Messiah? How do you prove that? These particular verses don't say, but others do. Take a look at these:

In Thessalonica:

> Now when they had passed through Amphipolis and Apollonia, they came to Thessalonica, where there was a synagogue of the Jews. And Paul went in, as was his

custom, and on three Sabbath days he reasoned with them from the Scriptures, explaining and proving that it was necessary for the Christ to suffer and to rise from the dead, and saying, "This Jesus, whom I proclaim to you, is the Christ." (Acts 17:1–3)

In Rome:

From morning till evening he expounded to them, testifying to the kingdom of God and trying to convince them about Jesus both from the Law of Moses and from the Prophets. (Acts 28:23)

All the same words are there—explaining, reasoning, proving. This is what Paul does. But do you see how he does it? He does it "from the Scriptures," "from the Law of Moses and from the Prophets." The story really couldn't be clearer: He opens the Bible, explains it, and calls on people to respond to what it says.

That's what we are called to do as preachers, too. We're called to expose the Word of God—the Scriptures—to our listeners. It's not about dividing up into camps or taking on labels. It's about following the instruction we see in Scripture concerning preaching and following the example we see in Scripture of other preachers. Time and time again the pattern is clear: They read God's Word, explain it, and call people to respond to what it says. Call that what you like; we call it *expositional preaching.*

God's Word at the Center

If everything we've been talking about is true, both of God's Word and God's Word preached, then it's no surprise that Christians throughout history have made the preaching of the Bible the centerpiece of their church's lives. We should do the same. Preaching has always typified Christians. It has always been at the center of their faith and at the center of their churches. In the earliest days of the church, in fact, that emphasis on the preaching of the Word was nothing short of scandalous. Christians were slandered as being "atheists" because the focal point of their faith was the spoken word rather than statues and figures of their gods.

If we're honest, the centrality of the preached word is still scandalous today. Nobody calls us "atheists" because of it, but they do chafe at the fact that in an age where the visual dominates and dialogue is king, Christians still expect one another to sit and listen as one man speaks to them for an extended period of time. And then to top it off, there's no Snap Poll at the end to register your opinion on the matter! But regardless of what people want or even *think* they need, the truth is that they need to hear the Word of God being opened and explained and applied to their hearts and wills. And that happens through expositional preaching.

Because of that, it seems self-evident that the preaching of the Word should stand at the center both of the public services of a church and at the center of the church's life as a whole.

Think about this: what is the focal point of your church's main public service? What do people walk away remembering? What does everything lead to and flow from? For some churches it's the music or a dramatic skit or a performance of some kind. For some it's the Lord's Supper or baptism. We would argue, though, that the center of a church's main public service—the most attention-demanding element in the service—ought to be the sermon. In fact, the sermon should be the one thing that shapes everything else in the worship service. The form of the service, from its songs to its Scripture readings to its prayers, should flow from and be shaped by the text of Scripture that's about to be expounded. Of course some elements should regularly be included in our public assemblies regardless of the sermon text—baptism and the Lord's Supper, reading of Scripture, prayer and singing, confession of sins, and encouraging one another in the faith. But precisely what specific encouragement comes during a given service, or which particular sins are confessed, or which aspects of God's character we focus on in our prayers and songs should all be informed by the main passage of Scripture that's going to be preached to the congregation. When that happens, the whole service comes together like a laser beam, and the truth of Scripture is applied powerfully at every point of the church's time together.

Sometimes, it's argued, making the sermon the centerpiece of our worship services demands too much of those who attend. They're not used to sitting under one man's voice for so long. We can certainly sympathize with that argument. Listening to a sermon may take more energy than watching a baptism or participating in the Lord's Supper. But a lack of attentiveness is not a virtue in Christians, and it's also not something that's "just human" for us to work around. In fact, the ability to engage with the preached Word of God is one of the things we as pastors should teach our congregations and should come to expect of them. There's a story of an old Puritan minister, a member of the Westminster Assembly, who was interrupted in the middle of his sermon:

> A few days before his death, when he was preaching [at Gregory's church], a rude fellow cried aloud to him, "Lift up your voice, for I cannot hear you:" to whom Mr. Vines replied, "Lift you up your ears, for I can speak no louder.[5]

Perhaps we as preachers should be *more demanding* of our listeners instead of "meeting them where they are" in their Internet-ravaged, television-shredded, 140-character-only, lopped-off-at-the-knees attention spans. That doesn't mean we should preach poor sermons and tell them they have to listen. But it does mean that perhaps we should teach the Christians God has placed under our care that they must *work* at listening to the sermon even as we work at preparing and preaching it. As another Puritan, Thomas Watson, said, "When we come to the Word, we should think within ourselves, 'We are to hear God in this preacher.'"[6]

Mark Ashton, of St. Andrew the Great in Cambridge, England, has put it well.

> There are few more encouraging noises for the preacher than the rustle of Bible pages among the congregation when he announces his text. He should draw comfort from that, more than from sounds of approval for what he is saying during the sermon. A faithful congregation will draw faithful preaching out of their pastor. Conversely, it is very hard to persevere as a faithful teacher of the Word of God to a congregation that does not want to have it taught to them. To some extent congregations get the preachers they deserve, because preaching is a two-way process: the attitudes of the preacher and congregation must unite in a humble hunger for God's Word.[7]

The centrality of the sermon in the church's services should be felt, too, in the life of the congregation as a whole. Both in the run-up to the Sunday morning sermon and in the outflow of the rest of the church's events throughout the week, the truths expounded from God's Word on Sunday morning should be evident and agenda setting. So, for example, both of us plan our preaching schedule well in advance, and we even print a card that gives sermon texts and titles for weeks and months to come. In that way our church members can see what's coming on the following Sunday morning and spend the previous week reading and meditating on that portion of Scripture. Interest is piqued, questions are raised, and the heart is prepared to come expectantly to hear the preaching of the Word. At Third Avenue Baptist, where Greg pastors, the church organizes its home group meetings around the prior Sunday's sermon. The discussion in those groups is geared toward a gritty, personalized application of the text that was preached.

It's, without saying, too, that when the preaching of God's Word shapes the agenda of the church's life as a whole, the congregation begins to learn the importance of protecting the pastor's schedule so that he has sufficient time to prepare to preach. Every church needs to understand what the Bible teaches about its leaders, especially about the central role that God has committed to ministers of the Word of being preachers and teachers of that Word. Too many pastors find themselves unable to give themselves to preparation for the ministry of the Word because they are too busy waiting tables (Acts 6:2). Other leaders in the church and the congregation as a whole need to have their expectations set. They need to understand that the sermon is the center of the pastor's responsibility. If we're honest, we should admit that practically everything else could be done by other qualified leaders in the church, but the main teaching of the church is the particular task of the preacher. Not only so, but it is the central need of the church, too. Those overlapping centralities—the need of the church and the task of the preacher—should be clearly understood and owned by the congregation as a whole. Not only will that prevent confusion and discouragement, but it will also encourage the spiritual growth of the church.

That, after all, is what we're aiming for, isn't it? We want to see the members of our church grow in maturity. We want to see them learn to love God more, to love His Son Jesus more, to love one another more in Christ. We want them to be spiritually *alive*. That's what God's Word does when it is preached. It gives life. It convicts, it encourages, it challenges, and it awakens faith.[8] Those, therefore, are the things we expect to see when we expose the Scriptures to our people and make the Word of God the center of our churches' lives—not because we are such particularly effective public speakers but because the Word of God is particularly and uniquely powerful.

CHAPTER FOUR

What Preaching Does

Think for a minute about the sermons preached in churches all over the world this past Sunday. What do you imagine they were about? What topics were addressed? What questions were asked? What exhortation was given? How many of the sermons preached from pulpits around the world this past Sunday do you imagine cut against the grain of the surrounding culture? How many of them do you imagine simply *reinforced* the surrounding culture?

A few years ago, the Methodist writer Bill McKibbens wrote an article in *Harper's* magazine entitled "The Christian Paradox: How a Faithful Nation Gets Jesus Wrong." In that article, McKibbens wrote about the preaching he had heard in evangelical megachurches. "It looks so much like the rest of the culture," he said. "In fact, most of what gets preached in these palaces isn't loony at all. It is disturbingly conventional." He went on:

> The pastors focus relentlessly on you and your individual needs. Their goal is to service consumers—not

communities but individuals: "seekers" is the term of art, people who feel the need for some spirituality in their (or their children's) lives but who aren't tightly bound to any particular denomination or school of thought. The result is often a kind of soft-focus, comfortable, suburban faith. A *New York Times* reporter visiting one booming mega-church outside Phoenix recently found the typical scene: a drive-through latte stand, Krispy Kreme doughnuts at every service, and sermons about "how to discipline your children, how to reach your professional goals, how to invest your money, how to reduce your debt." On Sundays children played with church-distributed Xboxes, and many congregants had signed up for a twice-weekly aerobics class called Firm Believers.[9]

Abdication of leadership is as much leadership as godly initiative-taking. If you fail to steer a boat, it simply flows downstream with the current, liable to all the eddies, rocks, and sandbars in the river, with no way to avoid them. Too many churches today have preachers who look to the culture around them not simply for the most effective methods of communicating their message but for the most effective message to be preached. Not a few churches—and that includes many "evangelical" churches—have tracked so long and so closely with the culture that they have become indistinguishable from it.

Preaching for Effect

Christian preaching, though, has at its heart the desire to make a change, to say something the world does not hear from anywhere else and does not even *want* to hear. It's not that Christian preachers are *looking* for ways to be contrarian. It's that the message we have been given to preach is the countercultural, status quo challenging, and offensive declaration that the human race is in rebellion against our King, and that our choices are to be judged for that rebellion or to accept love and forgiveness from His hand. Jesus knew the message He was giving His apostles to preach was not one that would win applause for them. "Do not think that I have come to bring peace to the earth," He said. "I have not come to bring peace, but a sword" (Matt. 10:34). What the apostles preached was going to cause the world to react against it precisely because it was cutting against the grain. It was a message that was seeking not just to invite people to think on a few things, to meditate on this or that idea, or to give a bit of food for thought. It was a message that was aiming for change.

Christian preaching seeks change. It cuts against the grain of surrounding culture, it challenges presuppositions, it convicts of sin, and it calls people to put their faith in Jesus Christ. It calls them to change direction. All the logical arguments and careful illustrations we use in our preaching are not there simply for artistry; we use them in an effort to have an effect on those who listen. After all, our whole salvation as Christians hangs on the fact that we heard God's voice calling us to repent and believe, to turn from one way of life to another. A change needed to happen, and that change was effected through our hearing of a message. When we preach, we should preach for that same effect in others, too.

One example of this idea of "preaching for effect" comes in the instructions for preachers that are given in the *Westminster Directory of Public Worship*. Here's what those pastors advised:

> In dehortation, reprehension, and publick admonition (which require special wisdom), let him [that is, the preacher], as there shall be cause, not only discover the nature and greatness of the sin, with the misery attending it, but also show the danger his hearers are in to be overtaken and surprised by it, together with the remedies and best way to avoid it.[10]

Do you see what they're saying there? Go ahead and explain to the people the nature and greatness of a particular sin. Show them the misery that comes along with it and the danger they face if they are overcome with it. But don't stop there! Show them also how to remedy that sin, how to fight against it, and how to avoid it! Of course, much in that quotation could be dismissed as mere moralism if it were divorced from a proclamation of the gospel. But preaching for effect in people's lives in no way necessarily undermines the sheerness of God's grace proclaimed in the gospel. In fact, the working out of the gospel in our lives *requires* that sin be carefully considered and countered.

The preaching of the Word of God is not a passive activity. It's not a mere meditation that stimulates the mind and goes no further. No, when we preach, we preach for change. We preach for effect. In everything—from the way we introduce our sermons, to the way we illustrate our points, to the way we bring everything down to the conclusion—we preach with the goal of spurring believers on in their maturity in Christ and of awakening nonbelievers to their need for the Savior. In a word, that answers that we preach with two main aims, to *edify* and to *evangelize*.

We Preach to Edify

The most extended treatment in the New Testament of what the Christian gathering should be like comes in 1 Corinthians 11–14. Paul says that his chief concern is that everything "must be done for the strengthening of the church." Throughout 1 Corinthians, this is Paul's main standard for deciding what should be done and what should not be done in the congregation. If that's true, then this same standard of usefulness in edification should especially be applied to what we have said is central to the life of the church—preaching. When we preach, we preach to edify.

What does that mean? What, specifically, should we be hoping to see in our churches as a result of our preaching? In 2 Timothy 4, Paul gives what he expects to be his final charge to young Timothy, whom he had left to lead and edify the church in Crete. It's an extraordinarily solemn charge, backed by the weightiest and most glorious truths Paul knew: "I charge you," he says, "in the presence of God and of Christ Jesus, who is to judge the living and the dead, and by his appearing and his kingdom: preach the word" (vv. 1–2). That exhortation doesn't come out of nowhere. In the previous few verses, Paul had already reminded Timothy of the power of the "word," by which he meant "the sacred writings," the Scriptures. Timothy himself knew, from his own experience, the power of the Scriptures. He had been acquainted with them and their power since his childhood, and he knew they "are able to make you wise for salvation" (1 Tim. 3:15). So now Paul charges him to remember that power and unleash it in his congregation.

In the course of encouraging Timothy to preach the Word, Paul lists four main ways those Scriptures are "profitable" in the life of the church. Look at 2 Timothy 3:16: "All Scripture is breathed out by God and profitable for teaching, for reproof, for correction, and for training in righteousness." This statement from Paul gives us a good, detailed idea of how we should pray for the preaching of the Word to edify our congregations. When you preach the Scriptures, the Scriptures will teach, reprove, correct, and train in righteousness. Let's consider each of these effects the Scriptures have in a church's life.

The words Paul uses in 2 Timothy 3:16 are not chosen at random. In fact, they divide rather neatly into two categories. Scripture is useful for doctrinal instruction, both positively and negatively, and it is useful for ethical instruction, again both positively and negatively. Taken together, all that provides a pretty comprehensive map of what is required to edify a church and build Christians up in Christ. We all need to be instructed both in doctrine and in the Christian life, and we need that instruction not only to be positive, showing the way forward, but also sometimes negative in character, showing us where we have gone wrong.

The first two words Paul uses, *teaching* and *reproof*, have to do mainly with doctrinal instruction. To "teach" is to explain the Scriptures, to instruct a congregation in what they say and what they mean. Paul uses the same word in Romans 15:4 when he says, "Whatever was written in former days was written for our instruction." Part of our task in edifying the church through the preaching of the Scriptures is to instruct our congregations in what is true about God and His ways. As people sit week after week under our preaching, their understanding of God ought to be built up and improved so that they know better what the Scriptures say about Him.

The corollary to that, of course, is that the Scriptures—and our preaching of them—are profitable for "reproof." The word appears only here in the New Testament, but where it shows up in other Greek literature, it means something like "an expression of strong disapproval." In other words, it means to confront and show the falsehood of wrong ideas about God and His ways. One of the surprising things you learn as a pastor is how many wrong doctrinal ideas the members of your church have picked up throughout their lives. From books they read, television they watch, even just through their own presuppositions, every congregation has imbibed wrong ideas about God, and therefore they need a pastor who will gently but firmly open the Scriptures and specifically contradict false doctrine.

The second set of words Paul uses here, *correction* and *training in righteousness*, refer primarily to ethical concerns. Part of edifying a congregation involves teaching them what it means to live in accord with the Gospel. The word *correction* was used in several different ways in ancient Greek. The initial meaning of the word was "restoration" or "improvement." It was what you might do to a city or a building that had fallen into ruin. From that meaning, though, arose the idea of "restoring" or "improving" one's ethical character and behavior. That is apparently the meaning Paul uses here. Scripture is useful for restoring a Christian's ethical character that has fallen into disrepair. If "reproof" has to do with confronting and refuting doctrinal error, "correction" has to do with confronting and refuting ethical error.

"Training in righteousness" is the positive counterpart to "correction." Most commonly it had to do with the "upbringing" or "raising" of a child. It was the combination of formative discipline and character development that parents would use to bring a child into productive adulthood. That kind of "training up" to "maturity" is a common theme in Paul's writing. In 1 Corinthians 14:20, for example, he tells Christians that they should not be "children in [their] thinking" but rather "mature." In Ephesians 4:13, when he's listing Christ's gifts to the church (including preachers and teachers!), he says that the end goal is that we should "all attain . . . to mature manhood, to the measure of the stature of the fullness of Christ." What he is telling Timothy, therefore, is something similar. His preaching ought to be aiming at building up Christians; it ought to be contributing to their maturity in Christ, as the teaching of a parent "trains up" a child to full maturity.

Paul's charge to Timothy here about the efficacy and power of Scripture is comprehensive. As the Scriptures are opened and preached, lives are impacted and built up on every level. The effect is broad and profound. People are instructed in right doctrine, protected from error, taught what it means to be mature in Christ, and corrected when their lives deviate from that standard of maturity. Preaching is not just a delivery of information, nor is it just for nonbelievers. We preach to edify the saints.

But that's not all.

We Preach to Evangelize

The basic meaning of the word we translate as "preach"—
kerusso—is "to make an official, public announcement" of something. It was something the herald of a king or emperor might do,
whether to announce the king's presence, to make known one of
his judgments, or to give some news to the people. That's the word
used most often of both Jesus' and the apostles' preaching. Matthew
opens his account of Jesus' ministry by saying that "Jesus began to
preach" (Matt. 4:17). Jesus Himself makes it clear to His disciples in
Mark 1:38–39 that His purpose was to preach. Pressed by crowds
who knew that He had power to heal, Jesus told Peter, "Let us go
on to the next towns, that I may preach there also, for that is why
I came out. And he went throughout all Galilee, preaching in their
synagogues and casting out demons."

The apostles, too, are said over and over to have preached in
the sense of heralding some news. That's the task Jesus gives to His
disciples in Matthew 10:7, "Proclaim as you go, saying, 'The kingdom
of heaven is at hand!'" In Acts 8:5, Philip goes down to Samaria and
"proclaims" or "preaches" Christ to them. That's exactly what Paul
does, too, immediately upon regaining his sight; he "proclaimed
Jesus in the synagogues, saying, 'He is the Son of God'" (Acts 9:20).
Later, in defending his ministry of preaching, Paul argues that it is
exactly the act of preaching that God uses to save people from their
sins:

> For since, in the wisdom of God, the world did not know
> God through wisdom, it pleased God through the folly
> of what we preach to save those who believe. For Jews
> demand signs and Greeks seek wisdom, but we preach
> Christ crucified, a stumbling block to Jews and folly
> to Gentiles, but to those who are called, both Jews and

Greeks, Christ the power of God and the wisdom of God.
(1 Cor. 1:21–25)

"We *herald* Christ crucified," Paul says. We make Him known to a world that does not yet know Him.

Kerusso, however, is not the only word that lies behind our word *preach*. Perhaps even more to the point is the fact that *preach* often translates the word *euangelizo*, "proclaim good news." That's the word Jesus used to sum up His ministry in Luke 4:43, for example: "I must preach the good news of the kingdom of God to the other towns as well; for I was sent for this purpose." The phrase "preach the good news" there is actually one word in the original Greek— *euangelizo*. "Preach the good news" is the dominant phrase, too, in the book of Acts. It's what the believers did after they were scattered by persecution (Acts 8:4), and it's what Paul and Barnabas did as they traveled from city to city (Acts 14:7, among others).

Given all that, one of the most important things we do when we stand to preach is *herald the good news of Jesus Christ*. We make Christ known, and we make known the good news that salvation is to be found in Him. Just as Christian preaching should edify believers in Christ, it also ought to call those who do not yet believe to do just that. We should preach to evangelize.

That doesn't mean, of course, that every sermon needs to be, in its whole, an evangelistic sermon, aimed primarily at unbelievers. We've already seen that one of the main purposes of preaching is to edify those who are already believers. But Jesus taught us that every text of Scripture ultimately points to Him (Luke 24:27), so the gospel ought naturally to lie at the center of every sermon we preach. Even beyond that, though, much of our preaching could probably benefit from a careful consideration of our text, our sermon points, and our illustrations from the perspective of non-Christians.

There are a few reasons why that kind of perspective would be good for us and our churches. For one thing, keeping the perspective that there will likely be nonbelievers listening to your sermons will actually be more edifying for Christians who attend because it will help you remember *why* you're speaking about a particular point. When you preach about the Trinity, for example, keeping in mind that non-Christians are listening will keep you from simply "checking the box" and instead will lead you to think about why the Trinity is important and how you could best explain its importance to someone who is brand-new to Christian thinking. When you do that, you actually help *Christians* understand those doctrinal points better, too, which reminds them of the importance and the applicability of God's Word, gives them fresh reason to praise God, and helps them, too, learn to engage with non-Christians around them.

I (Mark) spent some of my younger years as an agnostic. Because of that experience, I have learned through the years the value of trying to describe and defend biblical truth from a materialistic, naturalistic perspective. I know from my own years as an unbeliever what it means to have a mind full of inadequate, unbelieving presuppositions, and that has helped me through the years in knowing how to place a truth before someone for consideration, how to position it and deploy it, how to present it so that it most sharply challenges bad presuppositions. Most of the time, that's the kind of work we're going to have to do with the non-Christians in attendance at our churches. We're going to have to find a way to grab their attention with what we're saying instead of assuming they're naturally going to be interested in what we have to say. Because of that, I often make a point to address non-Christians directly. So, for example, when I (Mark) was preaching on 1 Corinthians 8 and began to discuss Paul's teaching about our knowledge being guided by love, I addressed non-Christians in the congregation:

> My friend, if you're here as a non-Christian this morning,
> I wonder how this is sounding to you. Have you realized

you weren't made to care about only yourself? For that matter, you weren't even made to care about yourself primarily and supremely. In the same way that we were made naturally dependent on our parents for generation and our earliest survival, and on a spouse of the opposite gender sexually, so we were made to be spiritually dependent on Someone Else, on God Himself. But, according to the Bible, we have each sinned and separated ourselves from God. We have rejected Him by choosing to be our own lords, and this self-centeredness leaves us open to the certain judgment of God, the right judgment of God, who will one day judge us. We are made in His image, and in judging us, He will display His glory by vindicating His own character.

That's not all I said to non-Christians, of course. Later on in the sermon, I presented the gospel more fully. But I pray that some who were there found something in that paragraph to think about, perhaps something they'd never thought about before and that would lead them to think of spiritual truth in a new way. I pray that they were unsettled in their unbelief and that they heard something the Holy Spirit would use to convict them of self-dependence and sin.

Brothers, never be afraid to address non-Christians directly in preaching. They generally know who they are, and they're not offended when we do that! Time and time again both of us have had non-Christians tell us after sermons that they appreciated being addressed publicly. It's not embarrassing for them. On the contrary, it let them know, they said, that they were welcome in our meeting, that we had something specific to say to them, and that we cared enough for them to spend some time talking directly to them.

The Word Will Accomplish Its Purpose

In Isaiah 55:11, the Lord makes a staggering and heartening promise: "So shall my word be that goes out from my mouth; it shall not return to me empty, but it shall accomplish that which I purpose, and shall succeed in the thing for which I sent it." When God speaks, His Word will accomplish what He intends it to accomplish. That's what it means to be omnipotent! That's also why we can be certain that the preached Word of God will succeed in its purposes of edification and evangelism. The Holy Spirit uses the preached word to give spiritual life to those who are spiritually dead, and He uses the preached word to conform God's people more closely to the image of Jesus. As preachers of the Word, we should have no less confidence in it than God Himself does. When we preach we should do so with the full conviction that God will accomplish His purposes through His Word. It will not return to Him empty.

PART TWO

Practice

CHAPTER FIVE

What to Preach On

How do you decide what to preach? It's a never-ending question for preachers because even after you're committed to preaching the Bible, it's not always obvious which text from the Bible you should preach to your congregation on any given Sunday. Should you skip around the Bible or follow it in order? Should you preach a paragraph, a chapter, a sentence, or a book?

Different men have answered those questions in different ways. Spurgeon wrote in his *Lectures to My Students* that he read his Bible and waited for the Holy Spirit to impress a text on his mind. Unfortunately, he said, sometimes the Holy Spirit waited until late on Saturday night to do the impressing, and sometimes He even switched things around on Sunday morning![11] Many preachers these days follow that model, choosing a verse or two each week from which to preach. Other men have set out to preach through the entire Bible from Genesis to Revelation, and a few others have even based their entire ministries on one particular book. One preacher named Joseph Caryl, a seventeenth-century Congregationalist minister, preached more than 250 sermons on the book of Job. He started in 1643 and ended almost twenty-four years later, in 1666![12]

Similarly, the size of the text from which men preach varies. Some preachers preach only a sentence or two at a time, or verse by verse. Samuel Medley, an eighteenth-century Baptist in England, often preached sermons on just one word from the Bible. D. Martyn Lloyd-Jones, too, preached a famous sermon on Paul's words in Ephesians 2:4, "But God!" Other preachers prefer to preach on a paragraph, a single story, a chapter, or some other self-contained portion of text. Some preachers go even further, preaching a single sermon sometimes on multiple chapters, a whole book, a whole testament, or even the whole Bible!

In this chapter we want to try to make sense of some of these questions and make a case that the best diet of preaching for your church would be one that makes its way through entire books of the Bible—in both testaments and in all the different genres of the Scripture. Once again, we're not saying that this is the *only* way to think about a long-term preaching schedule. But in our experience this is a plan that tends to teach Christians to read the Bible, to study it for themselves, and to understand better how it fits together.

Preach through Entire Books

Both of us have based our preaching ministries largely on the practice of preaching straight through various books of the Bible. Neither of us does that with *every* book of the Bible; some of them simply don't demand that kind of progression the way others do. Psalms, for example, could certainly be handled in this way; it has a definite structure, and people can learn from preaching it progressively. But it is also made up of 150 discrete units, each of which can be preached on its own terms without losing most of what the psalmist was trying to convey.

That's not true of most of the books of the Bible. Most of the books of Scripture are organized such that one chapter builds on the previous one and lays groundwork for what's coming in the next one. The narrative books—Genesis, Exodus, the Histories, the Gospels—are *stories*, in which events follow one after another to create a whole. Similarly, the books of the Law and the Epistles of the New Testament are tightly organized, logically flowing discourses; they are full of "becauses" and "therefores" that only carry their full weight when they're understood in relation to what is said around them. The Prophets, too, build their messages one expanding piece at a time so that their books become most powerful when they are understood in their entirety.

Many Christians—and those who preach to them—treat the Bible as if it's a collection of wise sayings, the order of which doesn't matter very much. It's as if all of Scripture is the book of Proverbs or the sayings of Confucius. But most of the Bible isn't like that at all. God inspired each of the books of the Bible with a certain internal logic and order. He inspired narrative and argumentation and prophetic cases against His people. The books build to climaxes, and they have elegant twists embedded here and there within them. Part of our job as preachers, therefore, is to help our people see the beauty of Scripture. We're not just looking for "nuggets of wisdom" buried in useless iron ore; we want our people to see the majesty of the whole, and preaching through entire books helps us open their eyes to Scripture's beauty.

Now of course it's possible to drop into a book—whether Law, Prophets, Gospel, or Epistle—and be faithful to the context of the text you're preaching. But an extra power comes to bear when you have brought your congregation along from the beginning of the book and then find yourself at one of the mountain peaks of that book. I (Greg) recently preached a series through the book of Judges. We took eleven weeks walking through it and toured one disaster area of a chapter after another! Now I could have dropped right into the book and preached the story of Samson, for example, as a one-off sermon, and I think I could have faithfully kept that story in its context and preached it well. But by the time our congregation got to the story of Samson, we had the whole weight of the narrative behind us—the darkness and heaviness and, frankly, the grossness of it—to help us understand what was really happening when God raised Samson up as judge of Israel.

Or take another example. You could drop into the book of Matthew and preach the story of Jesus' temptation in the wilderness, and you could do a good job explaining to your congregation what is happening in that story. But imagine if you were coming to Matthew 4 with all the weight of Matthew 1–3 behind you in your people's minds. For three chapters Matthew's been laboring through genealogy, narrative, and prophecy to show that Jesus is the long-awaited King of Israel; and finally in chapter 4, immediately after His baptism, Jesus takes up the *work* of being Israel's King. He confronts Satan and, acting as Israel's Champion, recapitulates each of their paradigmatic failures. Unlike Israel, He rebuffs Satan's temptation to demand comfort from God ("Command these stones to become bread," v. 3). He turns back Satan's demand that He try to force God's hand in caring for Him ("Throw yourself from the temple," v. 6), and He refuses to compromise with God's enemy in order to gain His kingdom ("Worship me," v. 9). You see? The narrative of Matthew builds step-by-step to that point when Jesus straps on His kingly armor and goes to war with Satan as Israel's Champion!

Another good reason to preach through books of the Bible in their entirety is that doing so forces you to preach on uncomfortable portions of Scripture. Few of us relish the thought of preaching on the Bible's texts about divorce. It's a touchy subject with multiple twists and turns in the teaching that are hard to get skeptical listeners to follow, and it's frankly easier just to go to John 3:16 again than to plant yourself for a few weeks in Matthew 19! And yet it is in Scripture, and we are called to preach the whole counsel of God to our people. That's where preaching entire books helps. After Matthew 18 comes Matthew 19. After 1 Corinthians 5 comes 1 Corinthians 6, and if you've established a pattern of preaching straight through books, you can't avoid them.

That has lots of good effects in our preaching and in our larger spiritual lives. For one thing it works hard against any fear of man that lurks in our hearts. One of the most crippling diseases for a preacher of God's Word is a fear of saying hard things from the pulpit—a blanching at the thought of preaching something that might offend and a resulting tendency to stay away from hard passages of the Bible. Preaching through entire books works against that fear and tendency because it forces us to preach those hard passages when they appear. In fact, it can help turn our sinful fear of man against itself—think ju jitsu!—because we won't want to face questions about our lack of courage if we skip from Matthew 18 to Matthew 20!

On the other hand, preaching through those books also protects us from being "blamed" for preaching hard passages at particular times. If you just skip around the Bible preaching what you think the congregation needs to hear, when exactly do you decide to preach on Jesus' teaching about divorce? The week you hear about a troubled marriage? The week after one of your church members, or their daughter, files for divorce? See, the trouble is that when it comes to those touchy passages, there's *never* a Sunday when you can preach them without *somebody* in your congregation thinking you've chosen *this* Sunday because of *them*. If your practice is to preach through entire books, though, you can lessen that danger considerably: "Sister Susan, no, I didn't preach this sermon because your daughter filed for divorce last week. I've been preaching through Matthew for three months, and we just happened to be in Matthew 19 today. Maybe you should send her this sermon, though? It might be helpful for her."

Not only that, but preaching through books forces you as a preacher—and therefore your church as well—to grapple with passages of Scripture with which you're not already familiar. As a result, you learn new things; you grow in your knowledge of God and His Word; and you mature as a Christian and as a pastor. If you skip around the Bible in your preaching, you will likely gravitate toward passages you already have thought long and hard about, passages you know a lot about already. We'd bet you're not likely to skip over to 2 Kings 14:7, for instance, and preach on King Amaziah's slaughter of ten thousand Edomites in the Valley of Salt and his renaming of Sela as Joktheel. Who would? Give me *John* 14:7 any day! But God inspired 2 Kings 14 for a reason, and the story of Amaziah's disobedience to God is part of the whole counsel of God that we are to preach to our people. Preaching our favorite passages, or the texts with which we're most familiar, means that our growth as preachers and even as Christians will be stunted. There are treasures unknown in the text we encounter as we preach through books.

Preach from the Whole Bible

We hinted at this point in the last paragraph, but we as preachers are called to preach the whole Bible to our people. If people sit under our preaching for any length of time, they should eventually hear us preach from a good cross-section of the entire Bible. That doesn't mean we should start in Genesis and end in Revelation; many men have done that, and it could be a fine idea sometimes. In our ministries, we have made it a practice to preach systematically through the various genres of Scripture and to move back and forth between the two testaments as we do so.

The Bible isn't all the same. It contains poetry, narrative, tightly reasoned argumentation, apocalypse, lists, numbers, law, biography, letters, wisdom, prophecy, and other genres, too. And of course, it's also made up of two testaments, the Old and the New. All of that, in its own way, is useful for our people; they need to hear from all of it over a given period of time. Both of us therefore have adopted a certain method for trying to make sure we preach from all the different parts of the Bible over a short period of time. Here's how we do it.

The Old Testament can be divided into five different genres, or categories if you prefer: Law, Histories, Wisdom, Major Prophets, and Minor Prophets. Similarly, we've divided the New Testament into the categories of Gospels and Acts, Pauline Epistles, and General Epistles and Revelation. With those categories in mind, we try to bounce back and forth through the categories and between the testaments. Here's how it looks:

Law	Gospels and Acts
Histories	Pauline Epistles
Wisdom	General Epistles and Revelation
Major Prophets	
Minor Prophets	

A preaching schedule for a year might look something like this: I pick a book of the Law, then a Gospel, then an OT book of history, then a Pauline Epistle, then a Wisdom book, then a General Epistle, then a Major Prophet, then another Gospel (or perhaps Acts), then a Minor Prophet, then another Pauline Epistle, then a different book of the Law, and so on. If your preaching series are ten to thirteen weeks in length, that lineup you've just read could stretch over about three years. If your series are generally longer, you could be looking at half a decade or more. Here, for example, is a list of the sermons I (Mark) preached at Capitol Hill Baptist Church over the first four years of my pastorate:

- Mark in 13 sermons
- Ezra in 4 sermons
- 1 Thessalonians in 7 sermons
- Ezekiel in 4 sermons
- Overviews of the General Epistles (1 sermon per book) in 9 sermons
- Proverbs in 5 sermons
- Mark 1:1–3:6 in 9 sermons
- Deuteronomy in 5 sermons
- 1 and 2 Timothy in 6 sermons
- 1 and 2 Chronicles in 4 sermons
- 1 John in 5 sermons
- Joel in 4 sermons
- Mark 3:7–6:6 in 6 sermons
- Song of Solomon in 2 sermons
- Overviews of the Old and New Testaments (1 sermon each) in 2 sermons
- 1 Timothy in 3 sermons
- James in 5 sermons
- Joshua in 5 sermons
- John in 11 sermons
- Overviews of the Major Prophets (1 sermon per book) in 4 sermons
- Titus in 6 sermons
- Overviews of the Wisdom Books (1 sermon per book) in 5 sermons
- 1 Peter in 13 sermons

The point here is not the length of the series but that, over a reasonable amount of time, our congregations are being exposed to the entire map of God's Word, instead of 250 sermons on Job! No, they're not getting every word of the Bible, but they are hearing us preach narrative, prophecy, law, gospel, apocalypse, epistle, argumentation, and genealogy. They're hearing us preach from both the Old and the New Testaments. They're learning how the Bible fits together, and in the process our hope is that they learn to appreciate and understand all those genres better.

So, how long should your series be? It's hard to say anything with certainty, but the benefit of using a structure like we've just described begins to break down if you preach five years in Deuteronomy. For that reason we prefer to make our series something like three to six months long. Sometimes we make it through entire books (even long ones) in that period of time, and other times we just take a portion of a book over that time period. When I (Greg) first came to Third Avenue Baptist Church, I preached the first thirteen weeks on the book of Matthew, but I only made it through the first seven chapters. Then the next fall, I picked up Matthew again and preached from Matthew 8–13 in another fourteen sermons. In the meantime I preached a number of other books in series of different lengths. Here's the schedule for my preaching ministry through my first few months at Third Avenue:

- Matthew 1–7 in 13 weeks
- The whole book of Genesis in 5 weeks
- The whole book of Titus in 3 weeks
- The whole book of Judges in 9 weeks
- The whole book of Hebrews in 11 weeks
- Five different Psalms in 5 weeks
- Matthew 8–13 in 11 weeks
- The whole book of James in 7 weeks (I broke the OT/NT pattern here!)

At that rate I think it will take me one or two years' worth of preaching to make it through the whole book of Matthew. I think it's good for me to preach the book in shorter series, and to take my church to other books in the interim. That way, their minds don't grow cold and bored, and their attention is renewed when we move to a new book.

Preach from Both a High Altitude and a Low Altitude

Did you ever see the video *Powers of Ten*? It's an old film that starts with a picture of a couple lying next to each other in the grass, and it tells you that you are looking at them from ten feet above the ground. Then the camera zooms out to one hundred feet, then a thousand feet, then two miles, then twenty miles, two hundred miles, two thousand miles, twenty-thousand miles, two-hundred thousand miles, two million miles, and so on. The earth disappears eventually, and you find yourself staring at the solar system, then the Milky Way, then a thousand galaxies. Then, the camera begins to move *in* by powers of ten. Eventually the couple on the grass comes back into view, but the camera keeps going until you're looking at a single cell on the guy's hand, then a molecule, then an atom, then an electron, and so on. It's a fascinating video because depending on your altitude, you see and understand different things.

The same thing is true for the Bible. Many preachers have the idea that the only appropriate altitude, or frame of reference, for preaching is one verse at a time, or perhaps at most one paragraph. Preaching at that level is fine and good. In fact, a short paragraph or self-contained story is probably the most natural level at which to preach.

On the other hand, there is often much benefit for a congregation when a preacher does something different and gives them either a broader or a narrower frame of reference than what they are used to. In fact, we think it is probably a *good* idea to vary your altitude in your preaching ministry, to preach some series that take paragraphs as texts, some series that take individual verses, and some that take chapters or multiple chapters or even entire books. I (Mark) tried to make it a point through the first few years of my ministry to preach what I call an "overview sermon" on each of the sixty-six books of the Bible as well as overviews of the New Testament, the Old Testament, and the entire Bible. I'm glad I did that. Those overview sermons have turned out to be some of the most useful sermons I've preached for my congregation because they give a snapshot of entire books and the message those books are laboring to get across.

Of course preaching from small units of text has advantages, and both of us try to do that on a regular basis. When you are dealing with only a few verses, you can draw out nuance and meaning at a very gritty level. Every word can be considered and opened up; prepositions, adjectives, and connecting words become fountains of meaning. The drawback to that approach is that over time your congregation can have their eyes so close to those individual texts that they lose sight of where they've come from and where they're going.

Similarly, preaching larger pieces of text, or whole books has both advantages and disadvantages. When you have only forty-five minutes or an hour to preach the whole book of Isaiah, you're necessarily going to miss things. You're going to gloss over whole sections of text with a sentence or two. But we think the advantages of an approach like that make it worth doing sometimes. When you preach a book in one or just a few sermons, what you're doing is taking a step back from its details to consider the thrust of the whole book. Think again about Isaiah, for instance. Most people tend to think about Isaiah as a massive bowl of undifferentiated judgment spaghetti, with a messianic meatball thrown in here and there (Isa. 9; 11; 53). But if you look at the book as a whole, you see that it's really more like a sword than a bowl of spaghetti. It has a shape, a weight, a point, a feel—all of which will be easier for your church to grasp if you preach it at a higher altitude than if you were to preach it verse by verse over several years. I (Greg) preached the whole book of Isaiah in three sermons, for example, one of which was on thirty-eight chapters at once! That experience most definitely challenged me and made me wish at times that I wasn't moving so fast. But on the other hand, people still tell me they remember the shape and weight and feel of Isaiah because of those sermons. They've learned to "wield" it because they were able to take in the whole from a high altitude.

Besides, it's not as if you only get one shot to preach each book of the Bible. My (Mark's) plan has been to move over the course of my ministry from a generally higher altitude in my preaching to a generally lower one. So I preached a sermon on the whole Bible, then on the New Testament, then on the Gospel of Luke, one chapter at a time. Maybe in a few years, if the Lord tarries, I'll go back and preach it again a paragraph or two at a time. If that happens, that will be something like *four times* that I've preached through the book of Luke (if you count the times I preached "through" it when I preached through the whole Bible and the New Testament). I'm just preaching through it at varying altitudes and learning new things every time I do.

On the other hand, I (Greg) don't have such a structured plan. Even now, in the first few years of my ministry, I'm preaching some books at a high altitude and some at a low altitude. That helps my congregation, I find, not to get too frustrated with either approach. Those who prefer verse by verse exposition are more willing to learn happily while I preach through Genesis in five sermons if they know I'm going to be returning to a closer look at Matthew in the next series. Over time I hope my people are learning to see the Bible in a fully textured and three-dimensional way—as a whole Book, full of whole books, full of whole sentences, in which *every word* counts.

Plan Your Preaching Schedule in Advance

The famous third-century preacher John Chrysostom told his congregation in His third sermon on Lazarus and the rich man, "I often tell you many days in advance the subject of what I am going to say, in order that you may take up the book in the intervening days, go over the whole passage, learn both what is said and what is left out, and so make your understanding more ready to learn when you hear what I will say afterwards."

We think that's a great idea, and we both try to follow that practice in our own churches by publishing a card that gives our preaching schedule—texts and titles—for the upcoming months. Doing something like that offers a number of benefits. First, like Chrysostom said, it gives your people time to read the passage in advance, to let the Holy Spirit begin to work in their hearts with the themes of that text, and to prepare their hearts to hear the Word of God preached on Sunday. That, in turn, can create a unique sense of excitement in the church. The people come with thoughts of their own, questions and insights about the text; and your words in the sermon are then able to interact with and catalyze with the thoughts they already have. Publishing a preaching schedule will give your people another tool for talking with their non-Christian friends and family about spiritual things. People take those cards, highlight or circle a particular sermon title they think a non-Christian friend might be interested to hear, and then hand it to that person as an invitation to come hear that sermon.

Sometimes people ask us if we think planning a preaching schedule so far in advance could squelch the Holy Spirit. What if something comes up in the life of the church that begs to be addressed? What if you get sick? What if something happens in the world such that your planned series seems out of place all of a sudden? Good questions all. But we don't think planning a schedule in advance squelches the Holy Spirit.

For one thing we don't think the Holy Spirit only moves "in the moment." Of course He does that sometimes, but that's not the only time He does it. The Holy Spirit also moves and directs months in advance when we are planning a preaching schedule. Both of us have been amazed at how people in our congregations have been impacted by a particular sermon or series in specific and time-sensitive ways. That's not because *we* planned for that to happen. On the contrary, we believe the Holy Spirit worked it all together in His providence. Take a look, for example, at this church card from Capitol Hill Baptist Church for the fall of 2001, which included September 11, 2001.

9/11/01 Sermon Card
September-December 2001

WHEN BAD THINGS HAPPEN
2 studies in Habakkuk
Sept 9   **Questions**
    Habakkuk 1-2
    Preacher: Jamie Dunlop
Sept 16   **Confidence**
    Habakkuk 3
    Guest Preacher: Bert Daniel

THE QUEST...
8 studies in the Psalms
Sept 23   **for Peace**
    Psalm 4
Sept 30   **for Justice**
    Psalm 5
    Preacher: Greg Gilbert
Oct 7   **for Security**
    Psalm 46
Oct 14   **for Forgiveness**
    Psalm 130
    Guest Preacher: Timothy George
Oct 21   **for Salvation**
    Psalm 2
    Guest Preacher: Bruce Ware
Oct 28   **for Mercy**
    Psalm 78
Nov 4   **for Holiness**
    Psalm 93

Nov 11   [see below]

Nov 18   **for Wisdom**
    Psalm 111

NAKED & NOT ASHAMED:
AN EVANGELICAL THEOLOGY OF SEX
A special symposium, by R. Albert Mohler, Jr.

Nov 11   **The Mystery of Marriage**
    Genesis 2

4:30 PM   **Reproductive Technologies**
    & Contraception

6:30 PM   **The Family and the Culture War**

Nov 12
7:30 PM   **Homosexuality:**
    Does Gender Matter?

WHAT THE FUTURE HOLDS
5 studies in Revelation
Nov 25   **The Man Who Saw the Future**
    Revelation 1:1-20; 22:6-24
Dec 2   **A Throne**
    Revelation 4-5
Dec 9   **A Lamb**
    Revelation 7; 14:1-5
Dec 16   **A Storm**
    Revelation 8:1-5; 11:15-19
Dec 23   **A City**
    Revelation 21:1-22:6

WHO HOLDS THE FUTURE
2 studies in Isaiah's prophecy
Dec 30   **The Sovereign God**
    Isaiah 6
    Guest preacher: John Folmar
Jan 6   **The God of Judgment and Mercy**
    Isaiah 7
    Preacher: Andy Johnson
    * AM Communion

That preaching schedule was made months in advance of the terrorist attacks in New York and Washington. Nothing was adjusted; nothing was changed in the aftermath of the attacks. But look at God's provision for this congregation right in the heart of one of the cities that came under attack: "The Quest for Justice," "The Quest for Security," "When Bad Things Happen: Questions and Confidence." The Holy Spirit was planning, even months before, to feed His people with truth from His Word that would impact their lives and their needs directly and specifically in the aftermath of—and even in *advance* of—a world-shaking event.

Not only that, but adherence to a preaching plan doesn't have to be slavish. Mark tends to stick to a preaching plan more doggedly than I (Greg) do. If Mark gets sick or something else intervenes, the church card is what the church card is—even if it means skipping a sermon in a series. I, on the other hand, have been known to pull all the sermon cards from our pews and print another batch.

We both have the same approach, more or less, to holidays. We both *try* to plan series in which the sermons that land nearest Christmas and on Easter won't be utterly weird—though Mark preached once on Christmas Day an entire sermon on death! But we don't insist that Christmas be from Luke 2 and Easter from Matthew 28. On Christmas Day 2011, I'm scheduled to preach on James 5:13–20, the prayer of the righteous for the sick. For Easter 2011, though, I shifted some things around so that I'd be preaching on Hebrews 8 rather than Hebrews 6. That was in the expectation that we would have an unusual number of visitors in the congregation who would attend church only infrequently, and I wanted a text that would have the gospel itself as the main point.

However you end up doing this, and however tightly you stick to a plan once it's made, the point is that planning your preaching schedule well in advance can give your people a good tool both for their own spiritual growth and for evangelism.

So, how do you decide what to preach? Well, as we said before, everything should be done for the edification of the church. We would argue that preaching through entire books, preaching from both testaments and all genres of Scripture, preaching from varying altitudes, and publishing in advance what you're going to preach will best accomplish that goal in the long run.

CHAPTER SIX

Sermon Preparation

A good friend of ours—a coffee snob if ever there was one—once said that when he goes into Starbucks, he orders a "triple grande, two-pump, low-foam, extra hot, low-fat, regular-syrup, vanilla latte." No kidding, that's his drink. Those who know him will not be surprised! Truth in advertising, mine's not much better. It's a "Grande Tazo Chai tea, unsweetened, with a little steamed milk on top." Mark's is . . . "milk. What do you mean what kind of milk? Just milk."

God bless him.

Giving preachers advice on how to prepare sermons is a little like telling them what "their drink" should be at Starbucks. It's deeply personal! So is sermon preparation in many ways, and every preacher does it somewhat differently. For example, I learned most everything I know about preaching from Mark, but you'll notice in this chapter that we don't do everything exactly the same way. We don't even *think* about some parts of sermon preparation in exactly the same way. That's inevitable, really, and probably a good thing. God calls a lot of different kinds of men to be preachers, and that creates a magnificent richness in the life of His church around the world.

We also hope you'll realize that entire books have been written and seminars taught on the mechanics of sermon preparation. Many of those books and seminars are exceedingly good, and we doubt there's much we can do in a chapter like this to match all of that. So we're not going to try. This chapter, therefore, should not be understood as a comprehensive guide to sermon preparation. Nor is it a comprehensive guide to biblical exegesis or to hermeneutics or to biblical theology.

On the other hand, we are also convinced that sermon preparation is a hard, time-consuming process, and that many preachers do not give themselves as fully as they should to that work. In this chapter, therefore, we want to show you a little of what we do in preparation for preaching, and perhaps even give you some ideas that will make your times of preparation more fruitful. You'll notice that we don't do everything in exactly the same way, but what we are both aiming for—most fundamentally—is to understand the text and then explain it and apply it to our people's lives.

Understand the Text

That's the first step. If you're going to expose God's Word to your people, naturally you have to start with understanding what your text says and what it means. If you mess that up—if the meaning of the text is muddled in your mind or if you're convinced of a *wrong* understanding of the text—your sermon will misfire badly. For that reason the most important part of sermon preparation is to make sure your understanding of the biblical text is deep, solid, and as comprehensive as possible.

Read It

Start with reading it. Both of us read the text we're going to preach multiple times in the previous week. Mark even uses the text as a part of his daily devotional time, reading it and meditating on it alongside any other readings he is doing. That's not to say that you have to be reading the text with the same intensity you will when you really start preparing for the sermon. Probably, in fact, you *shouldn't* read it with that kind of intensity. Just read it devotionally, and let it affect your heart; see what the Lord does with it in your own life. That could be wonderfully helpful to you as you prepare to present the text to your congregation.

One practice we both have found helpful in understanding the text is reading it in multiple translations. Whether it's by having an assistant sit and read the text to me in one translation while I stare at it in another (Mark), or just doing it myself (Greg), it's helpful to see how other Christians have translated the underlying Greek or Hebrew. Sometimes, of course, they get it wrong, and therefore you have to be careful before you make a particularly colorful translation the main point of your teaching! But on the whole it's helpful. Sometimes ideas are rendered more clearly by one translation than by another. Sometimes just the repetition of the same ideas in different words can jar your mind into new thoughts and new insights. The point, however, is simply to spend a good deal of time letting the text roll around in your mind, and reading it in different translations is a good way to keep the roll going!

Diagram It

Once you begin preparing in earnest, you should turn your full attention to understanding every detail of the text. That doesn't mean simply the meaning of every word and preposition and the archaeological background of every town name. Perhaps even more important is to understand the flow of the text. Why does this sentence follow that sentence? Why on earth does Jesus start talking about *that* right after He's been talking about *this?* How does this paragraph set that paragraph up, and where is Paul going with this whole train of thought?

One thing we find helpful in this process of understanding the flow of a text is diagramming it. There are many different methods of diagramming, and even the two of us do it slightly differently. Some prefer to do it in the original languages; others in English. Some like to mark the part of speech of each word, and others don't. I (Mark) generally type the text into a word-processing document. I don't copy and paste it; the act of typing it is helpful in flagging for my mind phrases and relationships between phrases that the eye can miss when I'm just reading. Once it's typed, I print the document out and then use colored markers to highlight various themes in the text. So every time I see Peter talking about perseverance, for example, I might mark it in green. Or when I see him mentioning something about atonement, I mark it in red. That color-coding system, which changes with every text, helps me see the tenor of the text. I can see at a glance how it flows from one idea to another, and that can help me as I'm working toward an outline.

My (Greg's) diagramming process is somewhat different. I don't type the text into a document but rather copy it with pen into a notebook. In the process I divide the text phrase by phrase, using lines to show how the various phrases connect to one another. As I move through the diagram, I find that I can get a clear picture of the "shape" of the text. Paul's writings, for example, are made up many times of one dependent clause after another. Diagramming helps me identify the main clause and then see more clearly how all the dependent ones relate to it. It can also help me see things that aren't obvious when I'm just looking at the text in paragraph form—when two clauses are parallel to each other, for example, or when even entire paragraphs hang on a single idea from a previous paragraph. I have found many times already in my preaching that a text will click into shape almost immediately when I diagram it, even if it looked really difficult the first time I read it.

Use the Original Languages

What about the original languages? Again, different preachers use the original languages to different degrees. Some guys actually take the originals into the pulpit and preach *from them!* Neither of us does that. We do use the original languages, but precisely how much varies from sermon to sermon. Both of us, for example, find ourselves using Greek more than Hebrew. Why? Neither of us is sure. Maybe it's that we both tend to preach longer passages out of the Old Testament than we do from the New Testament, so it's simply harder to spend as much time with a long passage of Hebrew as with a short passage of Greek. Even in the New Testament, though, our work with the originals varies from text to text. Some weeks I (Greg) read my whole text in Greek several times. Other weeks I find myself turning to the Greek only when I've run into some snag and *need* to look more deeply at it. Sometimes that clears up problems nicely; other times, frankly, it just translates the problem into Greek!

Ultimately, hardly a week goes by that we don't find ourselves in the original languages for at least part of our sermon preparation. The fact is, our English translations are for the most part very good, and it's rare to find them all wrong at the same time on something that *I* will be able to figure out on my own from the original language. And yet there's something wonderfully clarifying and insight generating about looking at a familiar text in a thoroughly unfamiliar way. One of the preacher's greatest enemies is familiarity: He thinks he understands a particular text because he has known its meaning all his life, and because of that he winds up missing its point when he preaches it. Looking at a text in the original languages helps minimize that kind of mistake.

Both Greek and Hebrew, for instance, tend to front-load their most important ideas, so the phrases that come at the end of our English sentences will often show up first in a Greek or Hebrew sentence. That's helpful if you've memorized a text in a certain way in English; when you read it in the original, it strikes your mind at a different and helpful angle. Not only that, but there are some texts that are the subject of raucous controversy, and many times that controversy turns on some point of Greek or Hebrew syntax or definition. You can certainly follow the arguments without knowing or engaging in any original language study, but the only way to get to the nub of the argument, formulate an opinion of your own, and then present your conclusion to your congregation is to have some facility with Greek and Hebrew. You don't have to know the languages fluently. I (Greg) have only what I call a "Bible-working" knowledge of both—just enough to use the software program BibleWorks! But as long as I remain humble about what I do and don't know—as long as I remember that there is a point at which you know just enough Greek to make a fool of yourself—it's helpful to me as a preacher to have that knowledge. It gives my understanding of the texts, and therefore my preaching (I hope), a depth and texture they would not otherwise have.

Use Commentaries . . . Eventually

Many preachers, we are convinced, retreat to commentaries on a text way too quickly. Sometimes even before they open the passage and read through it for themselves, they look at commentaries to find out what they *should* be seeing in the text when they finally read it. We think that's backwards. Part of the reason your congregation called you to preach to them is because they recognized in you an ability to read and understand *the Bible*, not just other people's opinions about the Bible.

We would encourage preachers, therefore, to spend a huge amount of time staring at the text for themselves, trying to discern the structure and the main idea on their own. Through reading it repeatedly, diagramming it, color-coding it, and meditating on it, you'll be able to understand its main contours and come to a good idea of how you want to teach it and apply it to your church.

So, when should you turn to commentaries? Essentially, we've found that there are two very good times to use commentaries. The first is when you run into a problem you just can't seem to break through. You've tried looking the phrase up in other parts of the Bible, turning it over in your mind to see if any new ideas come to light, even rethinking your diagram of the text to see if it clicks a different way; and it still doesn't make sense. That's a good time to go to the commentaries for help, and many times you'll find an insight there that will help smooth out the problem. Other times you'll just confirm that everyone else is as flummoxed as you about this particular problem, which is helpful in its own way! The second time commentaries are helpful is when you've come to a point where you think you have a good grasp of the text's meaning and you're getting ready to move toward a sermon outline. At that point we both find that it's a good idea to read a commentary or two just to make sure we haven't missed anything. So, for example, is there an Old Testament allusion you didn't notice or a logical connection between sentences you missed? Is there some important background information you weren't aware of, or have you been misunderstanding something? A good commentary on a text can help you discern all that before you move on to developing a sermon outline.

Move toward an Outline

Before you start thinking hard about application, you'll probably want to move toward an outline of the sermon. That will give you something to hang your application on, and it will also help you focus your application on the main points of the text.

The outline is a hugely important part of the sermon. It's what gives your congregation "handles" to grasp as you're preaching, and it helps them track along with you as you speak. Without a solid, clear outline, a sermon can easily become just a smooth, undifferentiated mass of words; and your listeners, not having any handles to hold to, will tune out until you're done. Not only that, but a good outline can serve to focus a sermon like a laser. Every point builds on and reinforces the last, until the whole sermon comes together powerfully to drive home one or two simple points. If you've done your outline well, your congregation should be able to write down only your main points and come away with a really good idea of what your sermon was about.

The Exegetical Outline

Both of us work our way toward a preaching outline *through* an exegetical outline. In other words, the first step of our outlining process is to put down on paper, in the plainest possible language, the main ideas of our text in the order they appear. That doesn't have to be complicated. Sometimes it's just a few sentences that give a snapshot of what's going on in the text. Here, for example, is the exegetical outline I (Greg) used recently in preparing a sermon on Matthew 12:1–21.

JESUS LORD OF THE SABBATH

- Pharisees' Challenge—self-righteous. It was their law, not God's.
- Jesus' Answer—You don't understand the law. Human need supercedes ritual law. Not an absolute analogy with Jesus' own situation; just a shot across the bow that their ritual-is-ultimate approach to the law doesn't make sense.
- Jesus' Answer—Higher authority supersedes ritual law. Temple was greater than Sabbath. Someone greater than the Temple is here.

MAN WITH WITHERED HAND

- Proof that Jesus is Lord of the Sabbath, like Matthew 9 is proof He can forgive sins.
- Pharisees' Challenge—Heartless. In fact, using Jesus' compassion against Him. Oily. Corrupt hearts; no compassion for this man. He's a tool for them.
- Jesus' Answer—Again, you know that's not the point of the law. You'll do good for a sheep, so how much more should you do for a man!
- Jesus' Answer—Heals him. Like Matthew 9. Point is Jesus' identity and authority.

FULFILLMENT OF ISAIAH PASSAGE

- Two points—Another claim for Jesus and also contrasting Him with Pharisees.
- Humble
- Gentle
- Victorious

You can see that in terms of wordage there's not much to it—even embarrassingly little, perhaps! Yes, there's a boatload of study behind those few phrases, and that outline obviously doesn't say everything I wound up preaching in nearly an hour-long sermon. But the point of that exercise wasn't to put every detail on paper. It was simply to give me a good snapshot of the main exegetical thrust of the passage. Your exegetical outlines may be more detailed than that; they may be less detailed. Just remember that your goal in an exegetical outline is not necessarily to include everything. It's to capture the shape and point and thrust of the text you're about to preach so you can move toward a preaching outline.

The Preaching Outline

Once you've nailed down an exegetical outline, you should move next toward a preaching outline—the actual points you'll articulate to your congregation when you preach the sermon. Sometimes you'll follow the progression of your exegetical outline almost exactly. Sometimes you'll deviate from it for one reason or another. Either way, now you are moving from a bare statement of what the text says and means to a more pointed "firing" of that text into the hearts and minds of your congregation.

One practice I (Greg) and my congregation have found particularly helpful is for me to work toward crafting a single sentence or two that will serve as the Main Idea for the sermon. Of course, because I intend to preach expositionally, that Main Idea of my sermon should also be what I think is the Main Idea of the text. Sometimes it's a statement and other times a question. But the purpose of it is really twofold. For one thing, it helps me in my preparation by focusing my thoughts and leading me to make sure I'm not putting anything extraneous in the sermon. Moreover, it gives my congregation one sentence that will call back to their minds the main thing we considered together. In a similar way, Mark will often conclude his pastoral prayer, which he prays just before the sermon, by praying through the points of the sermon (though he doesn't tell the congregation that's what he's doing). That, too, helps to orient people's minds to what is about to be preached from God's Word.

Ideally, a Main Idea sentence will have some rhetorical punch to it, and not be something flat and relatively boring. So, for example, instead of saying something like, "Jesus says spiritual life comes through Him, rather than through the Jewish ritual law," I'll present the Main Idea to my congregation like this: "Religion will kill your spiritual life. If you want spiritual life, you get it through Jesus, not through religion—and those two things are NOT the same!" Better, isn't it? Here's a list of some of the Main Ideas I used through my most recent series in Matthew:

- Matthew 8:1–22—This man Jesus is worthy of your trust. His is the kind of authority that deserves our faith, our commitment, and our very lives.
- Matthew 8:23–9:8—You want to be on this man's side. Every time, against every enemy, He wins.
- Matthew 9:9–38—Your religion, whatever it is, is hopeless. If you want to know God, be close to God, be loved by God, and be at peace with God, your only hope is Jesus the Messiah.
- Matthew 10:1–15—Evangelism is the natural heart response of a person who's met his King.
- Matthew 10:16–33—The world hates Jesus, and it will hate you, too, if you are His.
- Matthew 10:34–42—To be a Christian is to value Jesus Christ above everything—even if it means losing everything.
- Matthew 11—Who do you think Jesus is?

Some of those are better than others, but they all achieve the goal of stating the text in a provocative way, arresting the congregation's attention, and giving them something that will help them recall the main point of the sermon and therefore (if I've preached well) of the text.

Whether you use a Main Idea sentence or not, the next step is to decide on the points you'll use in the sermon itself. Sometimes those points will line up perfectly with your exegetical outline; sometimes they won't. Sometimes the best way to present a text to your congregation, for example, will be straight through the logical progression of the text. Other times the author weaves a number of themes and points together, bringing them up over and over again, and the best way to preach that text will be for your preaching outline to be more thematic. Either way, there are a few things that will help make your outlines more attention grabbing and memorable to your congregation.

I (Greg) had a preaching class in seminary in which the professor said that we should always try to make the points of our sermon "applicational." What he meant was that the points of our sermons should be in the form of imperatives because that will most engage the minds of our hearers and help them realize the relevance to their lives of what we're saying. That's probably good advice sometimes. There are plenty of times, though, when I wind up thinking that imperatives actually don't communicate the text in the best way, and it's better to use strong indicatives. The principle behind what my professor said, though, is certainly right: even if you don't use imperatives every time, you should strive to make the points of your sermon arresting in their own right. Imagine a sermon on Matthew 3:1–4:11, for example. You could certainly title the points of your sermon something like

1. John the Baptist
2. The Baptism of Jesus
3. The Temptation of Jesus

And that would be accurate. But you could also take it a step further and title them something more like

1. What God Demands
2. Who Jesus Is
3. What Jesus Wins

That's the same text under consideration, of course, but those points are more interesting and more arresting. They also point your listener to the main point of each of those stories instead of just identifying them, and they push the listener into thinking a little bit, too. "What? What does God demand? Who is Jesus? And what does He win? Tell me!!" Your goal ought to be to arrest attention from the moment you say the points. Create interest, raise questions, increase tension. Make people sit forward in their seats, anticipating how you're going to resolve all this.

Of course you have to be careful with the outline. You want it to be arresting, but in the process of getting there, you don't want to lose sight of the meaning of the text. Sometimes a dead-set determination to deal deftly in a dexterous display of alliteration will distract from the divine document more than it will duly declare its drift. Sophistication, style, and symmetry are swell in a series of sermon subjects (OK, OK—enough!), but the trouble is that sometimes your desire to find a word that starts with *P* will overshadow your desire to find a word that communicates the meaning of the text. The same is true of parallelism in sermon points. Sometimes it works. I think the "what, who, what" progression is pretty good in the example above. But sometimes it doesn't work at all. You just can't make it fit. When that happens, it's much better to go with what the text says and means than force the text into an outline that sounds good but is fifteen degrees off the actual meaning.

It's always a great feeling to get to the point of having a preaching outline. After you've done the work of exegesis, after you've understood the text and worked out the problems, and after you've brought it all down to a preachable outline, a huge part of the work of sermon preparation is done. Now you get to move on to the next huge part— application.

Meditate on Application

The first thing we should say about application is that you cannot do it until you have understood the text accurately. If you do, your sermon will leave people scratching their heads because the application will be off.

I (Greg) was driving to Chicago some time ago and caught a sermon by a radio preacher on my way. He was preaching on Isaac's blessing of Jacob and Esau in Genesis, and the point he was trying to draw from it—with great passion—was that parents should be effusive in their affection and praise for their children. One of his points was that parents should speak kind words to their children, just like Isaac did for his boys. Another was that it is important for parents to physically touch their children frequently, perhaps especially when they are speaking kind words to them.

Now all that may well be true. I try to do both those things for all my kids. But let's just be straight—that is *not* the point Genesis is trying to get across. Isaac's blessing has far more to do with God's promises to Israel and the chosen line from which the Messiah would come than it does any parenting principles. And sure enough, there was one thing in the text that threw this particular preacher off his stride, one thing he couldn't quite fit into his understanding of the text. It was that Isaac waited *so long* to speak like that to his sons. He should have done it earlier, the preacher said, when they were still children. Well, yes. Perhaps. And perhaps that oddity should have alerted him to the possibility that maybe parenting principles weren't really the main issue here.

I hope you can see my point. Trying to apply a text you haven't understood well is like hitting a nail at an angle. You can put all the raw strength behind it that you want, but it's never going to go in clean. You're going to leave people wondering where it came from.

Once you have the meaning of the text nailed, it's time to move on to application. It's time to meditate on why this text matters to your congregation, how it challenges their thinking and their behavior, how it undermines false gods they're clinging to, how it sets their eyes on Jesus and teaches them to rely on Him in the gritty details of their lives, how it uncovers and indicts sin and unbelief in their lives. If we really do preach for effect as we considered earlier, then application is a crucial part of our preaching. It is our job as proclaimers of God's Word not just to tell them what the truth is but also to tell them why the truth matters to them, and what the truth demands from them. You, as a preacher, do not just inform. You "reprove, rebuke, and exhort, with complete patience and teaching" (2 Tim. 4:2). In short, you apply.

Each of us has different ways of meditating on how a text applies to our churches. I (Mark) use a tool I call an "Application Grid." Once I've settled on a sermon outline, I create a grid with those points down the side and a number of categories across the top. Those categories ask various questions:

- How does the teaching in this point fit into the salvation-historical progression of the biblical story line?
- What does this text say to the non-Christian?
- What does it say to the larger society and to policy-makers?
- What does it say about Jesus?
- How does it apply to the individual Christian?
- Does it say anything in particular about issues of work or family?
- What does it say to my own local church, Capitol Hill Baptist Church?

Then I spend a good deal of time thinking, praying, and filling in the grid. Not every point of application I consider will make it into the sermon, but many of them do; and this grid helps me not to fall into the rut of preaching only to the individual Christian, which, in my experience of listening to preaching, is where most preachers tend. It forces me to think about how my text applies to other groups of people as well, not least to my particular local church.

I've also found that talking through application with a member of my church is helpful in stimulating thought. I've made it a practice over the last fifteen years to take a few members of my church to lunch on Saturdays and think with them through the application grid. Those are sweet times of fellowship, and they're also enormously productive. More times than I can count, the men with whom I'm having lunch have asked a question I hadn't considered, made a point I'd overlooked, or had a pastoral insight that hadn't occurred to me. Then, later, after I've written the sermon, I'll read it to a few friends in my study on Saturday night, and often there are women present who give me some of the best comments I receive.

My (Greg's) process of thinking about application is a bit different. I don't use an Application Grid, at least not one that's on paper. My way of thinking about application is to take a long "sermon walk." Most Saturday afternoons I go for a two-, even three-hour walk around my neighborhood if the weather's good or at the local mall when it's not. I take my iPhone with a Bible on it, a notebook with my outline written in it, and a pen. I walk, think, and pray. I've always hoped somebody would stop me and ask kindly, "What are you doing, young man? Oh? Preparing a sermon? Tell me about it." That's never happened, but I did have a guy once run out of his house yelling at me and demanding to know why I wrote his license plate number down. I tried to explain, but he seemed to be more relieved and slightly embarrassed than interested.

On that sermon walk, I think through the text I'm preaching and ask similar questions to the ones we mentioned above on the application grid. What is the burden of this text? Why does it matter for my church? What keeps people from thinking this way? What are the obstacles to doing this or to living this way? Why does this text or doctrine or truth matter *for Robert*? There's an important point: I almost always try to think of specific individuals in my congregation and think about why this text should matter to those people in particular. That practice helps remind me that I'm not preaching to the Internet but to a specific congregation, and it helps me, I think, to make applications that are more personal and trenchant. In the two or three hours I'm walking, I probably preach the sermon to myself in a hundred different ways. I chase rabbits in my head, I walk around in my own mind and heart, and I try to uncover my own motivations and fears and sins that are challenged by the text. And all the while I make notes in my notebook. By the time that walk is done, I have a good idea of where I want to go with the sermon, and I'm ready to put it on paper.

One last point on application for now: we encourage you to work toward having multiple "levels" of application in your sermons. Some applications will be long and involved because they will tap into the main thrust of the text and be among the one, two, or three main points you're hoping to get across in the sermon. Other times your applications will be shorter, one- or two-sentence exhortations that you fire into your listeners' hearts. Maybe it's because those applications are coming from a relatively peripheral point in the text; maybe it's because you have other applications to give. Either way, don't be afraid of those. Sometimes the most commented-on points in our sermons are those one-off, sentence-long applications.

Preach the Gospel

One crucial thing you should keep in mind through all your preparation—from understanding to outlining to meditating on application—is that your task as a preacher is ultimately and fundamentally to preach God's Word. "Yes, yes, you say, of course! That's what you've been saying through this whole book!" True, but we're making a more specific point here, and it is that one of our convictions as Christians is that every text of the Bible points finally and ultimately to Jesus Christ and His gospel. Every Old Testament text, as Jesus told us time and again, points forward to Him, and every New Testament text points either backward or forward to Him.

Jesus is the beginning, the center, and the end of every text in the Bible.

Because of that, your sermons should never be forty-five-minute morality lessons or best practices for living a better life. They should drive forward to the good news that King Jesus saves sinners through His life, death, and resurrection from the grave. In fact, we think that in every sermon you preach, you should include at some point a clear and concise presentation of the gospel. Tell people how they may be saved! I never want someone to come to my church, not just for a length of time but even for one single service, and be able to say they didn't hear the gospel of Jesus Christ. Brothers, you are not Jewish rabbis. You are not called to give sermons that merely tell people how to live rightly or better. Is teaching people to live rightly part of preaching the whole counsel of God? Yes, absolutely, depending on the text! Is that ever all there is to it? Absolutely not! One way or another, every text in the Bible points to Jesus, and you should follow where it points.

That doesn't mean you should simply tack the gospel onto the end of your sermons. We've all heard that—a sermon on marriage that really says nothing about Jesus until the last two minutes of the sermon, and then the gospel is just sort of duct-taped onto the end. That's not what we mean. What we mean is that the gospel should flow naturally and forcefully out of the themes and stories that make up the text you're preaching. It's vitally important that you let every text speak for itself; if you're preaching from the Old Testament, present that text with its own voice, and let it speak to your congregation with all its original force. But you also want to let those texts speak with their *full* voices, and that includes letting them say what they want to say about Jesus! In other words, you should not just preach each text in its immediate context, but you should also preach it in its context with reference to the entire Bible.

But how do you do that without it sounding contrived and forced? It has helped me in my preaching to know there are two different roads to the gospel from every text in the Bible, roads we should be on the lookout for in every sermon we prepare. One is the road of biblical theology, and the other is the road of systematic theology. Let me give you an example from a most unlikely text: I (Greg) recently preached a series on the book of Judges, easily one of the darkest, most hopeless books in the Old Testament, and probably further away from the gospel, salvation-historically, than any other book. I mean, how, for example, do you get to Jesus in a sermon about Ehud? When the text you're preaching is about a tricky, left-handed sneak who stabs a fat king and gets away because the guards are deterred by the smell, how exactly do you turn from that to the glories of Jesus? Or how do you do it from the story of the Levite and his concubine or the civil war in Israel? It's not obvious sometimes, but it can and should be done. And it can be done by following the roads of biblical theology and systematic theology.

Biblical theology has to do with the whole grand story line of the Bible. From Genesis to Revelation, the Bible tells a story, and from any given text you can always step into that narrative river and be swept pretty quickly toward the cross. Even in Judges you can get to Jesus easily by seeing how the book fits into the whole story. After all, the main point of Judges is the refrain, "In those days there was no king in Israel" (Judg. 17:6; 18:1; 19:1, for example). The book is an apologetic for godly kingship, even kingship rooted in the tribe of Judah. Follow that unfolding story line, and you quickly find yourself at King David and ultimately at King Jesus, "the Lion of the tribe of Judah, the Root of David" (Rev. 5:5).

Of course, you can't make that the main point of every sermon in the series. Even if you mention that story line in every sermon to be sure your people understand it, sometimes you need another road to the gospel. That's where systematic theology comes in. Throughout the Bible, there are certain themes that are easy to find. Sin, grace, sacrifice, and salvation, just to name a few, underlie every story in the Bible; and all of those themes find their highest expression in Jesus' death and resurrection. So when you're preaching from the Old Testament, find one or more of those themes and then turn strongly to the cross. In Judges, for example, human sin, broken covenant, God's grace and love, God's wrath, and His deliverance of His sinful people are all strong theological themes, and any one of them is a great way to turn your listeners' minds to Jesus and His work of salvation for His people.

It's easy to preach the Bible, especially the Old Testament, as if it were a book of fables—a series of stories that do little more than instruct us morally. But if we believe Jesus, we know those stories are doing much more than that; they are pointing us to Him. So whether we do it by following the story line or pointing out the themes, our job is to show our congregations how to see Jesus, even from the story of Ehud.

Write It Down

Once you have a good grasp of the text, the applications that flow from it, and the way it points to the gospel of Jesus, all that's left is to write it down. That's always the hard part for both of us, but it's also the crucible in which language takes shape. Mark Twain once said that "the difference between the almost-right word and the right word is really a large matter—it's the difference between lightning and the lightning bug." He's right, and the writing of the sermon is where the hard work of *getting the right words* is done.

The English language is a remarkable tool for communicating. There are so many words, each with its own shades of meaning that can change the whole tenor of a sentence or even make it strike the heart in a wholly unexpected way. Is there a difference, for example, between warning your congregation that they might *fall* away from the faith and warning them that they are in danger of *drifting* away? Perhaps not much, but the latter carries a connotation of neglect resulting in slow, almost imperceptible loss. It's not sudden like a fall, and if you're not careful, you can drift far away before you realize it's happening.

Be careful about the words you use. Work on them. Figure out precisely what you want to say and say it precisely. It's hard to do that on the fly while you're in the pulpit. Much better to do it on paper, beforehand, when you can try one word or way of putting an idea, reject it, and then try another. Your preaching will benefit from that discipline, and so will your congregation.

CHAPTER SEVEN

The Structure of a Sermon

———— ·《◦》· ————

Have you ever built a model rocket? Neither have we. But from what we understand of model rockets, it stands to reason that if you *were* going to build one, it would be really important to get all the pieces in the right places and working properly. If you put the rocket's nose on the side instead of on the top, the thing is not likely to fly. If the thruster is on the top rather than on the bottom, you'd probably get a nice fire but little altitude. Even if everything is in the right place but one part isn't working properly, the rocket isn't going to fly—at least not straight. If you want the rocket to fly, all the various pieces have to be in the right place, and they also have to be functioning properly.

A sermon is something like a toy rocket. If you want it to fly and accomplish its purpose, you have to understand something of the various pieces, you have to get those pieces together in good order, and you have to make sure each piece is functioning properly. In this chapter we want to consider five "pieces" of a typical sermon, give some advice about them, and make some comments about how they fit together to make a sermon fly. Those pieces are introductions, exegesis, illustrations, applications, and conclusions.

Introductions

Martyn Lloyd-Jones was a doctor before he was a preacher, and he often took his medical perspective into the pulpit with him. He thought of the people arrayed before him as his patients, and his task as a preacher was to give them medicine from the Word that would help heal them from their spiritual diseases. Lloyd-Jones thought highly of the usefulness of the first few paragraphs of a sermon. They were, he said, his first and best chance to win the attention of people who otherwise would not care what he was saying. Here's how he put it:

> I am not and have never been a typical Welsh preacher. I felt that in preaching the first thing that you had to do was to demonstrate to the people that what you were going to do was very relevant and urgently important. The Welsh style of preaching started with a verse and the preacher then told you the connection and analyzed the words, but the man of the world did not know what he was talking about and was not interested. I started with the man whom I wanted to listen, *the patient*. It was a medical approach really—here is a patient, a person in trouble, an ignorant man who has been to quacks, and so I deal with all that in the introduction. I wanted to get the listener and *then* come to my exposition. They started with their exposition and ended with a bit of application.[13]

I (Mark) think Lloyd-Jones is absolutely right. The introductions I often hear in otherwise good sermons are frequently underused.

Sometimes they are simply an invitation to turn to the text, which is really no introduction at all. Other times they're a story or a joke with only a tenuous connection to the sermon's main theme. Great things can be accomplished in sermons through introductions. Each preacher will develop his own style, of course, but introductions should not be thrown away as if they don't matter or are not spiritually useful. On the contrary, introductions form a kind of funnel for the congregation's interest. They draw together all the disparate and conflicting focuses that mark your congregation and pull attention to the themes you're going to be preaching on. Even more, sermon introductions are a good way to front-load application for the Christian and also to let non-Christians who are present know that they are welcome, and that they are heard.

What do I mean by front-loading application for the Christian? I don't mean that you should literally begin with all your applications. What I mean is that your congregation will be helped to listen well if they understand why the things you're saying are relevant to them. That relevance can be in any number of categories. It may be a challenge to their way of thinking, or an exhortation about their Christian lives, or a clarification of some doctrine. The sermon can matter to them in the sense of encouraging or comforting them as they come to understand God and His ways more, or it can matter in the sense of instructing them on what they ought to do. Whatever the *kind* of relevance, the point of an introduction should be to teach your congregation that they listen to sermons not just to pile up religious knowledge so they can win Bible Trivial Pursuit the next time they play! No, the reason we listen to sermons is to be instructed, encouraged, challenged, corrected, and spurred on in the faith; and sermon introductions can be a valuable way of setting that expectation right up front.

Any text of Scripture you handle in a sermon will have implications for people's understanding or feeling or doing, and if you start with just a taste of some of those implications—if you ask some of those questions or challenge some of those presuppositions up front—it will help your congregation pay attention. It will help them care about the sermon more than if you simply say, "Last week we finished chapter 7, and now we begin with chapter 8 verse 1." That kind of approach assumes a great deal of interest in the text; it assumes everyone present is waiting with baited breath to hear what you have to say about chapter 8. That may be true of your church; if so, never leave! In most churches, though, it's just not the case. People come into corporate worship with a thousand things on their minds—children, the in-laws, who's coming to dinner, how am I going to pay that bill, wow look at her dress, I need a nap, do the Cowboys play at 12:30 or 4:00—and if you don't arrest all those lines of thought right from the beginning, you'll probably never be able to corral them. A good introduction will offer the congregation a motivation to put their distractions on hold for a while and do the hard work of listening well to a careful biblical sermon, the kind of sermon that will help them mature both as a congregation and as individual Christians.

A second thing I try to accomplish with introductions is to involve non-Christians who are present and let them know that they are heard, that their concerns and questions and objections are being taken into account in the sermon they're about to hear. Generally, people who disagree with you will assume that the arguments and points you make are off because you don't understand something about them, their concerns, or their perspective. As a preacher and pastor, I genuinely understand that, and I would like to understand them. More, I would like to *show* them that I am preaching as someone who has at least *tried* to understand them.

Let me give you an example of what I mean. Here's a fairly brief introduction I (Mark) preached in a recent sermon on Mark 1:35–39, the passage where Simon Peter finds Jesus out praying early in a solitary place, and Jesus teaches His disciples that He had come to preach. My introductions are sometimes longer than this, sometimes more elaborate, and sometimes tie in better with the conclusion of the sermon. But I think this will give you a good idea of what I mean by involving the non-Christians in your congregation:

> *Enigma*, from the Greek word for "fables" and to speak in riddles, means something obscure or hard to understand, like an inscrutable problem or a mysterious person.
>
> It's amazing when you think about it that by far the most written-about person who has ever lived should be such an enigma to so many people. But there's no denying that He is. "I pray to Jesus for the good winds," said one Hindu girl, as she told me of a whole list of gods she prayed to. "I don't believe He ever existed," said another person. Even among those who revere His name, Jesus is often no more than a remote figure, comforting or forbidding by turns, depending on my own emotional state or sense of guilt. Historically we know a lot about who Jesus was in the plain sense of the question—a Jewish first-century itinerant Palestinian teacher. But in the deeper sense—*why* Jesus was—ah, now that is the enigma.
>
> Why did Jesus live? Why did He come? To meet felt needs? To be a shining example of personal spirituality? To teach the esoteric insights of the ages or the virtuous way to live?
>
> Why did Jesus come? At the time of Jesus' ministry, many different ideas were around. Many thought He had come simply as a rabbi. After all, He was addressed as "rabbi." He proclaimed God's law, taught in synagogues, gathered disciples, debated with the scribes, was asked to settle legal disputes, and even sat as He taught, the traditional rabbinic way of teaching.

Others saw His miracles and thought He had primarily come to perform wonders of healing and exorcism and the multiplying of food. Some saw Him as a reincarnated Old Testament prophet, others as someone who drove out demons by the power of the prince of demons. He was called a king, a glutton, a drunkard, a prophet, a criminal, a revolutionary, God, and a blasphemer. Why did Jesus come?

That's what the Gospel of Mark wants to tell us about this morning. Our text is Mark 1:35–39.

In that introduction my hope was to have helped both the Christians and the non-Christians listen well to the rest of the sermon. My intention was that Christians would not only be informed where the text was in the Bible but would also plant in their minds something of the significance of the issues raised in it. This text often has been preached as "follow Jesus as an example. Go off by yourself to have a quiet time, and make sure to have your morning watch early in the morning." I hope, though, that my congregation will come to understand that far larger issues are at stake here, that Jesus' very identity and purpose are tied up in how he answered Simon Peter's request to come see the crowds.

And for non-Christians listening, my hope was that they would hear and understand that this Christian preacher has some understanding of mystery, has Hindu friends, has conversations with non-Christians, and understands that people have various estimates of Jesus. And I want them to think these things *not* because I'm fundamentally concerned with what they think about me, but because I want them to be persuaded that they are going to hear a fair presentation of who Jesus is and who He claimed to be.

Exegesis

We've said this before, but it's worth saying it again: The foundation of every good sermon is a good understanding of the text it's expositing. That's true not just for the preacher in his preparation and actual delivery but also for the congregation as they listen. For that reason it's crucial that your sermon clearly explain what is going on in the text.

Preachers are tempted to err in their exegesis in two important ways—either by giving too much information or by giving too little. Either can be hugely detrimental to the power of a sermon to accomplish its purpose. Some preachers, on the one hand, are tempted to skip over the exegetical part of a sermon and move too quickly to illustration and application. It's easy to see the temptation of that approach. Congregations generally perk up when you make it clear that you're moving to application; they respond more and better. Heads nod, "amens" come. That doesn't happen so often when you're explaining the flow of thought in Romans 7. But doing the work of teaching is important nonetheless, not so much because your congregation will find the teaching scintillating but because the teaching of the text provides the foundation from which application can be launched. If you try to apply a text before your congregation understands it, the power of that application will be drained enormously. When the congregation can see clearly that application is coming directly from the meaning of the text, it impacts their minds and hearts with its full power.

The opposite error some preachers make is to give their congregations every piece of information they ran across in their study of the text. The meanings of Greek words, their etymologies, a list of all the other places in Scripture where a certain word is used, archaeological backgrounds of every place mentioned—all of it gets thrown into the discourse as if it's a Wikipedia article on the text instead of a sermon.

It's best not to do that. Instead, the portion of your sermon devoted to teaching should take as its singular goal to help your people understand the weight and balance of the text. You should certainly explain to them why Jesus answers this question as He does or why Paul follows up discussion of this topic with a discussion of that topic. But most of the time the particular etymology of the Greek word underlying that adjective won't be necessary for a congregation to understand the meaning of that text. Yes, it might add some color, or you might find it interesting, but it can also distract from the power of the text's main direction and thrust. I (Greg) preached a sermon some years ago, when I was much greener (!), in which I interrupted my explanation of a certain psalm to explain that when you're going to pronounce the Hebrew word *chesed*, you have to be careful to make a good, rolling guttural sound in the back of your throat! I'm not sure why I did that. It was a true point; I was and remain absolutely right about it. But it was also completely irrelevant to the point the text was making, and I was pilloried for it later when the church staff reviewed the sermon. In another sermon on the first chapters of Isaiah, I decided to fill my congregation in *with detail* on the political and geographical situation of Assyria and Egypt vis-à-vis Israel. It was all interesting to me, but it was utterly irrelevant to what God was saying in that text. I could have said what was necessary in two minutes rather than in twenty. That ended up being a seventy-five-minute sermon. It still embarrasses me to think about it.

A good, general rule of thumb is to include only those details necessary to illuminate the meaning of the text and drive its point forward and home. If certain detail doesn't do that, don't use it in the sermon.

Illustrations

Illustrations are easily some of the most abused parts of sermons today. Some preachers abominate them and don't use them at all. Others seem to think that sermons are composed only of illustrations. I (Mark) remember hearing a sermon some years ago in which a preacher gave a ten- or fifteen-minute illustration in a half-hour sermon. In all honesty it was a good story that he told well and convincingly. I remember the details of it even now. I remember the plot line of the story. In fact, I even remember some of the names of the people involved, and that's highly unusual for me. But here's the rub: I could not begin to tell you the passage of Scripture this brother was preaching on, or what his points were, or the spiritual impression of the text. I don't even remember the point he was illustrating with the story. All I remember is the story.

We're told by experts that we live in a narrative age. That may be true, but it also makes one wonder if there has ever been an age—knowing how humans experience time and memory—that *wasn't* a narrative age. When have people ever not liked stories? Stories involve us. We find stories in the Old Testament, extended images of marriage and adultery used in the prophets, Pharaoh's dreams and Nathan's parable of the rich neighbor taking the poor neighbor's only sheep. And of course, all the history of Israel comes down to us in stories—a set of characters in which action takes place over some period of time. It is only natural, therefore, that preachers communicate by using illustrations, not just in this age but in every age. Nevertheless, we need to take great care in using them. We need to make sure that our illustrations don't overwhelm the sermon, that they don't take too long, and that their own drama doesn't detract from the weight and thrust of the sermon as a whole. Illustrations are meant to illuminate not to obscure. Here, therefore, are a couple of pieces of advice about illustrations:

Illustrations don't have to be stories. Sometimes an arresting description of a scene will serve as a perfect illustration. It will bring a biblical story to life and impress on your hearers the importance of the scene. For example, in Hebrews 13, the author exhorts his readers to go "outside the gate" with Jesus. It's an image of the rejection that would come to Christians because of their allegiance to Christ. Now, in illustrating what the author means there, you could certainly tell a story about a time when you felt rejection because of your faith. But might it not be better, and even more arresting, NOT to tell a story but rather just to describe what the author of Hebrews would have been thinking when he wrote the phrase "outside the gate?" Here's how I (Greg) handled that passage when I preached on it. This is word for word from my notes:

> Have to understand what it meant to be "outside the camp," "outside the gate." Inside the gate you had holy ground, but outside was where filth and uncleanness were. Would have been obvious if you could walk up; Judah, Ephraim and their banners. But outside—That's where dead bodies were buried. It's where people relieved themselves. If you went outside the camp, you had to be ritually cleansed before you came back in. And all around, outside the camp, ramshackle huts—lepers who would wail, "Unclean! Unclean!" and run away lest the wind blow their sickness onto someone else. Same outside the city. That's where Jesus died—out there. Even Romans determined that crucifixion was too dirty to be done in the city. Out there, with the uncleanness. Astonishing thought, really, when you think about it, that life would be found in a place of death, that holiness and righteousness would be won in a place of the most revolting uncleanness.
>
> And know what? It's a good thing, too, because that's where I am. If you knew your heart, you'd cry out

"unclean, unclean" because you'd know that where you *belong* is among the graves and the filth. And yet it's exactly to people like me and you that Jesus came—to the unclean so that we may be clean, to the unholy so that we may be holy. Reverses infection. He suffered and died *outside the camp*, where I am, where you are. Don't run away, run *to* Him. GOSPEL Have to realize you're outside the camp, can't win righteousness. Praise God, we find life outside the gate, because that's where we are!

Good to remember when a Christian, too. When sin beats us down, when you find yourself dead spiritually. Jesus is not one who wants you to clean yourself up before you come to him. People say all the time, "Need to get things in order before I go to Him, talk to Him, before I serve Him." As if you should scrub and scrub because you're going to the King's throne room. O friend, if that's what you think, then you don't know Him! This is not a King who is afraid of dirt. This is a King with scars in His hand because He died outside the gate. This is a King who loves those who are dirty and filthy, whose natural place is outside the gate, and who know it, and who come to Him to take mercy from his hand. Dear brothers and sisters, if your sin is heavy and filthy in your life, go to Him; bow down; hand it to Him. It won't be a surprise to him. He suffered and died outside the gate, not to save those who have no sin but to save those who are *broken* by sin and cry out to Him for salvation.

See, there's no story there, but my hope was that an arresting description of what it meant to be "outside the gate" would set up the truth that Jesus loves sinners who realize they are hopelessly filthy. The description, not a story, set the stage for that point.

Be careful with personal illustrations. One modern habit that is especially problematic is the overuse of the personal illustration, the story of how you did something or spoke to someone. Start a sentence with "I was talking yesterday with . . ." and watch how your congregation tunes back in, how their focus comes right back to the pulpit! That's entirely normal and expected. There's nothing unusual about it because it's a change of pace, you learn something about the speaker, and there may be a little entertainment value, too. But for all their power, personal illustrations should only be used with the greatest of care. If you're a faithful pastor, you'll already have enough temptations to build a congregation too much around yourself and your own personality. In part, God has given you that personality to do just that—to be a winsome preacher of the gospel and to implore people to come to faith in Christ. But on the other hand, you must be careful not to allow your church to become the church of Mark or the church of Greg instead of the church of Jesus Christ. Use yourself sparingly, and never leave the impression that the church's life or health depends on you. Never leave the impression that you're the hero or the smartest, wittiest guy in the city. When you do use personal illustrations, make yourself a bad example sometimes—the person who said the *wrong* thing rather than the right thing, the person who is in desperate need of God's grace. If your illustrations only illustrate your goodness and brilliance, they have failed to illustrate the gospel of Jesus.

Application

One of the most common questions asked of us as expositional preachers is, "When you preach expositionally, how do you apply the text in the sermon?" First, we should note that behind this question, there may be many questionable assumptions. The questioner may be remembering expositional sermons he has heard (or maybe even preached) which were no different from Bible lectures at college or seminary. They may have been well structured and accurate, but they seemed to have little godly urgency or pastoral wisdom. These expositional sermons may have had little if any application. On the other hand, the questioner may simply be misunderstanding what application really is. There could have been a great deal of application in the sermons in question, but he may simply not have recognized it.

William Perkins, the great sixteenth-century Puritan theologian in Cambridge, instructed preachers to imagine the various kinds of hearers who would be listening to their sermons and to think through applications of the truth preached to several different kinds of hearts—hardened sinners, questioning doubters, weary saints, young enthusiasts; the list goes on and on.[14] Let's approach the question slightly differently, though. Many of us who are called to preach God's Word will surely know this already, but it will be helpful to remind ourselves again of this fact: *Not only are there different kinds of hearers, but there are also different kinds of application which are themselves all legitimately considered application.*

When I preach the Word, I am called to expound the Scriptures, to take a passage of God's Word and explain it clearly, compellingly, even urgently. In this process at least three different kinds of application reflect three different kinds of problems we find in our own Christian pilgrimage. First, we struggle under the blight of ignorance. Second, we wrestle with doubt, often more than we at first realize. Finally, we sin—whether through directly disobedient acts or through sinful negligence. All three of these problems we long to see changed in ourselves and our hearers every time we preach God's Word. And all three give rise to different kinds of legitimate application.

Ignorance is a fundamental problem in a fallen world. We have alienated God from us. We have cut ourselves off from direct fellowship with our Creator. Informing people of the truth about God is itself a powerful type of application and one which we desperately need. This is not an excuse for cold or passionless sermons. I can be every bit as excited (and more) by indicative statements as I can be by imperative commands. The commands of the gospel to repent and believe mean nothing apart from the indicative statements about God, ourselves, and Christ. Information is vital. We are called to teach the truth, to proclaim a great message about God. We want people who hear our messages to change from ignorance to knowledge of the truth. Such heartfelt informing is application.

Doubt is different from simple ignorance. In doubt we take ideas or truths familiar to us, and we question them. This kind of questioning is not rare among Christians. In fact, doubt may well be one of the most important issues to be thoughtfully explored and thoroughly challenged in our preaching. We may sometimes imagine that a little pre-conversion apologetics is the only time we preachers need to address doubt directly, but that's not true. Some people who sat and listened to your sermon last Sunday, and who knew all the facts you mentioned about Christ, or God, or Onesimus, may well have been struggling with whether or not they really believed those facts to be true. Sometimes people's doubt is not articulated. We may not even be aware of it ourselves. But when we begin searchingly to consider Scripture, we find lingering in the shadows questions and uncertainties and hesitancies, all of which make us sadly aware of that gravitational pull of doubt, off there in the distance, drawing us away from the faithful pilgrim's path. To such people—perhaps to such parts of our own hearts—we want to argue for and urge the truthfulness of God's Word and the urgency of believing it. We are called to urge on our hearers to the truthfulness of God's Word. We want people who hear our messages to change from doubt to full-hearted belief of the truth. Such urgent, searching preaching of the truth is application.

Sin, too, is a problem in this fallen world. Ignorance and doubt may be either themselves specific sins, or the result of specific sins, or neither. But sin is certainly more than neglect or doubt. Be assured that people listening to your sermons will have struggled with disobeying God in the week just passed, and they will also struggle with disobeying Him in the week they are just beginning. The sins will vary. Some will be disobedience of action; others will be disobedience of inaction. But whether of commission or omission, sins are disobedience to God. Part of what we are to do when we preach is to challenge God's people to a holiness of life that will reflect the holiness of God Himself. So part of our applying the passage of Scripture we're preaching is to draw out the implications of that passage for our actions this week. We as preachers are called to exhort God's people to obedience to His Word. We want people who hear our message to change from sinful disobedience to joyful obedience to God, according to His will revealed in His Word. Such exhortation to obedience is certainly application.

Of course, the main message we need to apply every time we preach is the gospel. Some people do not yet know the good news of Jesus Christ. Some people who have been sitting under your preaching may have been distracted, or asleep, or daydreaming, or otherwise not paying attention. They need to be informed of the gospel. They need to be told. Others may have heard, understood, and perhaps even genuinely have accepted the truth of the gospel but now find themselves struggling with doubt about the very matters you were addressing (or assuming) in your message. Such people need to be urged to believe the truth of the good news of Christ. And, too, people may have heard and understood but may be slow to repent of their sins. They may not even doubt the truth of what you're saying; they may simply be slow to repent of their sins and to turn to Christ. For such hearers the most powerful application you can make is to exhort them to hate their sins and flee to Christ.

In all our sermons we should seek to apply the gospel by informing, urging, and exhorting.

One common challenge we preachers face in applying God's Word in our sermons is that sometimes those who have their problems mainly in one area or another will think you're not applying Scripture in your preaching at all if you're not addressing their particular problem. Are they right? Not necessarily. While your preaching might improve if you do start addressing doubt, for example, more often or more thoroughly, it is not wrong for you to preach to those who need to be informed, or who need to be exhorted to forsake sin, even if the person talking to you isn't so aware of that need.

One final note. Proverbs 23:12 says, "Apply your heart to instruction and your ear to words of knowledge." In English translations the words translated "apply" almost always (maybe always?) refer not to the preacher's work, or even to the Holy Spirit's work, but rather to the work of the one who hears the Word. We are all called to apply the Word to our own hearts and to apply ourselves to that work.

Ultimately, Lloyd-Jones had it right again:

> We must ever remember that the Truth of God while meant primarily for the mind is also meant to grip and to influence the entire personality. Truth must always be applied, and to handle a portion of Scripture as one might handle a play of Shakespeare in a purely intellectual and analytical manner is to abuse it. People have often complained that commentaries are "as dry as dust." There is surely something seriously wrong if that is the case. Any kind of exposition of "the glorious gospel of the blessed God" should ever produce such an impression. It is my opinion that we have had far too many brief commentaries on and studies in the Scriptures. The greatest need today is a return to expository preaching. That is what happened in the time of the Reformation and the

Puritan Revival and the Evangelical Awakening of the 18th Century. It is only as we return to this that we shall be able to show people the grandeur, glory and majesty of the Scriptures and their message.[15]

Conclusions

Concluding a sermon can be one of the most difficult parts of preparing to preach. We have all heard sermons where the preacher seems to have a terrible time "landing the plane." He bounces it on the runway six or seven times in a row but always seems to take flight again just when you think he's going to hit the brakes. But "landing the plane" in a sermon is just as important as taking off.

Ideally we as preachers want the conclusion of our sermon to be weighty. We want it to bring the full weight and force of our message down, like a wedge, into the hardened sinner's heart, the complacent Christian's will, or the wounded saint's soul. It needn't be anything loud or dramatic and shouldn't be anything that would distract from the points we've been making from the Scriptures. It should simply drive those points further in with one final, heavy statement or question.

One of the best conclusions I (Mark) can recall was at the conclusion of a sermon on the crucifixion of Christ, from Mark's Gospel. Dick Lucas was preaching, and as he stood there, plain and still in the pulpit, meditating on the work of God in Christ, he finished the sermon in a voice both awed and simple: "Nothing more to be done. No barrier between God's love and you. As far as God is concerned all sins are put away. He will accept you if you come in Jesus' name, not on your own. If you come humbly in His name, you are *welcome.*"

And with the enunciation of the word "welcome," the warmth of God's acceptance of me in Christ thrilled and awed my soul once more. It wasn't just that one sentence. It was the way everything he had been preaching—about my sin, about Christ's love, about atonement and the cross and the wrath of God and substitution and Jesus' death—everything was summed up and encapsulated in that sentence, "If you come humbly in His name, you are welcome." And then it was the way all the blessings of the gospel, the great need of humanity to be reconciled to God, was summed up even in the last word, "welcome." It was a brilliant example of how the entire weight of the sermon came pressing down into the listeners' hearts in the last sentence, even the last word, of the sermon. It left us all not applauding the preacher but silently in awe of Jesus Christ.

That, finally, ought to be the goal of every sermon. If introduction, exegesis, illustrations, application, and conclusion are all working together perfectly, the result ought to be that the whole sermon leaves your congregation thinking not about your brilliance as a preacher but about the burden and message of the text you just preached. It all ought to line up to turn your hearers' eyes to Jesus— to spur them on to love Him, His Word, and His people more.

[CHAPTER EIGHT]

Delivering the Sermon

Is there anything quite like the few seconds right before you open your mouth and begin to preach? The music is done, everything is quiet, all eyes in the building are on you. You step to the pulpit, open your Bible, lay out your notes on the podium, . . . and pause.

Or at least I do. For just two seconds—maybe three—I pause before I begin speaking and let my eyes scan the congregation, maybe even make a split-second's eye contact with some people. It's not for effect, nor is it to try to gather attention the way a school-teacher might fall conspicuously silent when her class is getting restless. No, that tiny pause is for me. It's to remind myself why I'm there, to press into my own heart one last time the enormity of what I'm doing. "These people," I think, "belong to Jesus. They are His. He loved them, He spilled His blood for them, and He has put all the resources of omnipotence behind His determination to bring them safely home. And now, for the next hour, He's putting them . . . in my hands. To teach them and encourage them."

Richard Baxter, the Puritan preacher, said this: "I preach as never sure to preach again, as a dying man to dying men."[16] To stand before a congregation and open the Word to them is an action weighty beyond degree. It is not to speak down to them, as if we ourselves don't desperately need the grace we are holding out to them in our sermons. But it is to stand and speak as one who has found the cure for the deadliest of diseases and to implore our listeners to open their own eyes to that cure as well. It is a weighty and glorious responsibility.

We (Mark and Greg) have talked together about that responsibility—from the preparation of a sermon to its delivery—many times and at great length, and we agree that the best part of the process is actually delivering the sermon, standing in the pulpit and bringing all the preparation and all the writing to fruition in spoken words. It's a wonderful feeling! As wonderful as it is, though, that doesn't mean it's easy. Delivering a sermon is as much work, and has as many pitfalls, as preparing one; and many are the preachers who can prepare a manuscript to end the world and yet still don't seem able to deliver it with freedom and power.

To be perfectly frank, there's finally no way to *teach* a gift for preaching. As much as every other talent and every other spiritual gift, an ability to preach the Word powerfully is something God gives by His grace alone. Even so, all of us can improve in our delivery of God's Word. No one—not even the Spurgeons, Whitefields, and Pipers of history—are born with every tool for proclamation firmly clicked in place and finely honed. A preacher can always improve, no matter how gifted he is. In this chapter we want to consider some of the issues and questions involved in sermon delivery. As we do, we hope some of this will be useful to you in your labor, to improve your own preaching so that you will be better able to deliver God's Word to your church with clarity and power.

Manuscript or Outline?

Is it better to preach from a manuscript or an outline? In all my (Mark's) years of traveling and speaking on the subject of expositional preaching, it would be hard to recall an event where that question *wasn't* asked of me. I use a full manuscript in my preaching, usually running somewhere between ten and fifteen pages. With a few exceptions I put every word I'm going to speak on the page. As we talked about earlier in this book, I find that practice helps me to hone my words and present my ideas with the greatest possible force and precision. I love this description of Richard Baxter's preaching:

> The sand glass at his side measured the length of the sermon, which was never less than an hour, and his custom was to read it from a closely written manuscript. "I use notes as much as any man when I take pains," he said, "and as little as any man when I am lazy or busy, and have not leisure to prepare."[17]

"When I take pains." No kidding! Writing a manuscript is certainly a pain. It takes a long time, it's tiring, and it's tedious. But at least for me, the rewards far outweigh the pains. By the time I finish writing, and then read over the sermon once or twice more, I am deeply familiar with every line of it. I know where I am going with the sermon and what I want to say. I've chosen the words carefully, and each one, as far as I am able, is calculated to communicate God's Word with the greatest accuracy and force.

That doesn't mean, of course, that I stand in the pulpit and simply *read* my manuscript, as if I were giving an academic paper at an academic conference. No, I labor to *preach* the sermon with passion and conviction, to move the hearts and wills of my listeners so that they are spurred on to respond well to God's Word. It also doesn't mean that I stick slavishly to my manuscript and never say anything that wasn't prepared beforehand. That's just not my nature anyway! Several times in any given sermon, I'll "off-road" from my manuscript, whether it's with a thought that didn't earlier occur to me, or an extra bit of application, or just a humorous aside for no real reason at all. I don't want to be a wooden, word-making contraption standing behind the pulpit. I want to be a human being who knows and feels his need for a Savior and therefore the weight of what he's saying, but I want to be a *well-prepared* human being who knows and feels those things!

My (Greg's) sermon notes are nowhere near as long as Mark's. Where his run to something like thirteen or fourteen pages, mine are more like three or four. I don't write down every word I plan to say. In fact, it's probably more accurate to call my sermon notes "detailed outlines" than to call them manuscripts. Some parts of my notes are more scripted than other parts. I tend to manuscript application sections more than exegesis sections, for instance, unless I'm going to be working through a particularly tricky text. I also tend to manuscript tight theological teaching that requires more precision in language. I find that I tend to "off-road" quite a lot in my preaching, and I also tend to repeat ideas when I have a sense that they didn't stick the first time I said them. So a detailed outline allows me to work carefully with my wording, but it also creates some space for expansion and elaboration when I'm actually in the pulpit.

One of the things we've noticed, especially in young preachers, is that there's often a tension between accuracy and personality in the pulpit. When a guy takes a full manuscript into the pulpit, he tends to be precise in his wording but also somewhat wooden and chained to the manuscript. His sentences come out sounding very "literary" because the written word sounds different from the spoken word. You've probably noticed that as you've listened to preachers. When someone is just talking, sentences tend not to be very pretty. There are run-ons and fragments and reversals; sentences tend to be short and not elaborate. The written word is different. Sentences are more elaborately constructed with dependent clauses and rhetorical flourishes. They also tend to be longer and more freighted with adjectives and adverbs. That's fine, as far as it goes. The trouble, though, is that your listeners' minds are adept at picking up when you slip into *speaking* what are obviously *written* sentences—in other words, when you begin reciting. Think about the lines actors deliver in a school play; that's what it sounds like—slightly artificial no matter how much feeling you put into it.

So how do you avoid that? Some guys, of course, have no problem with it at all. They can take a full manuscript into the pulpit and sound like they're speaking entirely off-the-cuff. You'd never know they planned every line of it in advance. Other guys don't have that kind of natural ability, but they learn over time how to do it. They learn how it *feels* when they slip into a "literary" voice, and they learn how to adjust and come out of it quickly. One method that might help bring precision and personality together is this: Write out a manuscript. Work hard on the words. But then leave it at home. In other words, do the work of manuscripting, but then take an outline (of whatever level of detail) into the pulpit. Or, alternatively, just shrink your detailed manuscript into six-point font so it's there if you need it but too small to lean on for long. That way you've done the hard work of finding good words and images so that they're in your mind, and yet your mind can also do its work of translating those great words and images into something you'd actually say if you were just talking instead of reading or reciting.

In the end, the important thing isn't whether you use a manuscript or an outline. What's important is that you strive to be careful and precise with your language and at the same time to preach with conviction and passion and personality. "Logic on fire"—that's how Lloyd-Jones once defined preaching. "Light and heat" is how our forebears used to talk about it. They're all right. Leave out either one of those elements—light or heat, logic or fire—and you're left with something far short of biblical preaching.

The Density of Sermons

Again and again we are told today that sermons should be easier to understand than they were in the past—less abstract, more spontaneous, and shorter, with more stories from personal experience and allowing for more participation from those who are listening. All that is taken for granted by many preachers today. Of course there's something to be said for simplicity in preaching. And passion, boldness, and daring in preaching, when wed to the truth, are excellent! None of that should be disputed. But we'd argue that strong content—and a lot of it—is excellent, too! You want your sermons to be filled with content that will feed and nourish your people.

One of the ways preachers most frequently seem to discourage themselves is by believing everybody should remember every bit of what they preach. We put so much time into crafting every point, we think, and then a week later people have difficulty remembering what we said, and that's discouraging. So, we reason, let's give them less! Maybe they'll remember more of it!

If that's how you've been thinking, you need to drive that thought right out of your mind. The point isn't for your congregation to be able to recall, like human Google searches, every sentence or even every point you made. The point is for the Word to shape their hearts and minds and wills, and that can happen even if they don't remember the precise words or points you spoke. Think about it: What novelist writes a novel expecting that you'll remember every plot twist? That's not his goal; his goal is to bring you along in the story, to make you feel the weight of the story, and to affect you with it. Or think about advertising. What advertiser makes a commercial with the thought that you'll remember the ad's dialogue? Again, that's not their goal. The goal is to impress upon your mind the importance and desirability of the product so that you'll be more likely to buy it. They're in the business of shaping minds and hearts.

Christian preaching, of course, isn't precisely like either of those examples. There is a propositional, creedal content to the Christian faith that just doesn't exist for, say, Charmin Ultra. We want to preach that content, and over time we pray our people will remember it and use it in their lives. But don't fret when you realize your people aren't retaining everything you say; your words and the truth you present will still be working to shape them and mold them into the likeness of Christ. Besides, over time, the most important truths *will* stick, and they'll remember them. As preachers of God's Word, we simply want our sermons to be clear and our points to be accurate and firm. Much of the work we do on sermons is simply to prepare those points and then deliver them to those who have ears to hear.

I (Mark) assume that only about 20 percent of the adults hearing my sermons will get most of what I say. But that's fine. Those 20 percent who have an appetite that particular day are the ones I want to feed. People are used to news anchors and magazines and teachers who know more than they do; why shouldn't preachers be in that same category? As long as the gospel is clear to all, is it really a problem to make people reach a little for some of the things taught in the sermon? Does preaching sermons that are a little more demanding at points really make us remote, or intimidating, or unapproachable? I don't think so. If you're a remote, intimidating, unapproachable person, even your simplest sermon is going to be remote, intimidating, and unapproachable. And besides, maybe saying a few things that cause our people to stretch a little in their understanding will help them have confidence in us. Maybe it will give the most mature believers in our churches something else to learn from the sermon, and maybe it will attract the kind of people who show the maturity of valuing both love and knowledge.

"But what about the children?" someone will ask. Brothers, blessing parents will bless children. Helping mom and dad understand the gospel, to understand love, to think through what it means to be a good example and a bad example may all be concepts that are above some of the younger children in attendance at your church, but if the parents come to understand those things, they can teach their children. Besides, you'll do the children no good at all by teaching their parents only things they would have understood fully when they were ten years old.

I would encourage you, therefore, to preach sermons for adults. That doesn't mean your sermons should be complicated and difficult to understand. But they should be as serious and as weighty as life itself. A good rule of thumb is to assume that everyone who ever hears you preach is both very intelligent *and* very uneducated. In other words, assume they have never been taught about the Christian faith, but that they are fully capable of benefiting from a solid explanation. And then explain it to them. Don't simply assume your listeners are incapable of understanding or uninterested in what Scripture says. If you preach like that, yes, you might be assuming and even asking for a serious level of interest in your sermons. But why is that a bad thing? That's exactly the kind of expectation, seriousness, and interest you want to encourage in your church as they listen to the Word.

And that brings us to another point about sermon delivery.

The Tone of the Sermon

Too many evangelical sermons today smack of a smug triumphalism that is every bit as repulsive as a despairing defeatism. Christian sermons should certainly be suffused with confidence in the triumph of the conquering Lamb, but at the same time they should have about them an air of truth and realism about our cursed world. Sermons, like other aspects of our corporate worship services, should frankly acknowledge the difficulties of living the life of faith. Abraham, Moses, David, Jeremiah, Paul—all lived the life of faith, and they all struggled and suffered as they did. Jesus Himself was more confident of victory than anyone who has ever walked the earth, and yet He loved and patiently taught and retaught, and prayed and groaned and denounced and wept.

So what exactly is the appropriate tone for a Christian sermon? Here are five aspects of the tone we should desire in our sermons:

1. Our tone in preaching should be *biblical*. At its best our preaching should never smack of parties—Presbyterian or Baptist, Calvinist or Arminian, amillenial or dispensationalist. Rather, our sermons should always be obviously biblical, with any doctrinal distinctives we espouse clearly arising from the text. In that way the powerfully attractive thing becomes not membership in your party but rather faithfulness to God's Word and its truth. Just as the story of the Bible centers on God, so should our preaching. Sermons that are biblical will spend time considering who God is and what He has done. The gospel will naturally be central. We should be preaching not to draw people into one theological group or another but rather to draw them to Christ.

2. Our tone in preaching should be *humble*. If we are seriously contemplating God and His grace in our preaching, then prideful self-congratulation will find no place in our sermons. They will instead be marked by the aroma of grace. We'll be like the Salvation Army captain I once read about who gave this testimony on his deathbed: "I deserve to be damned. I deserve to be in hell. *But God interfered.*" If we truly understand God's grace, we'll never enter the pulpit thinking that we deserve to be there. Instead we'll know a deep sense of unworthiness before we bring God's Word, and a confirming sense of shame afterwards as we see how God uses His Word in people's lives, and as we consider how much better we're able to preach than to live.

3. Our tone in preaching should be *clear*. Biblical humility in no way comes from an uncertainty about the truth of our message. Too often today there is a wrong kind of timidity. We actually act as if we are scared that we may be understood. True humility, though, centered on God and His Word, brings a bold clarity. It is the humility of a herald who would not dare change the message of the King who sent him but who also would not dare to speak that message with anything but the firmest conviction of its truth.

4. Our tone in preaching should be *sober and serious*. In the beginning of his book *Counted Righteous in Christ*, John Piper laments the ungodly lightness of too many evangelical services today:

> The older I get, the less impressed I am with flashy successes and enthusiasms that are not truth-based. Everybody knows that with the right personality, the right music, the right location, and the right schedule you can grow a church without anybody really knowing what doctrinal commitments sustain it, if any. Church-planting specialists generally downplay biblical doctrine in the core values of what makes a church "successful." The long-term effect of this ethos is a weakening of the church that is concealed as long as the crowds are large, the band is loud, the tragedies are few, and persecution is still at the level of preferences.
>
> But more and more this doctrinally-diluted brew of music, drama, life-tips, and marketing seems out of touch with real life in this world—not to mention the next. It tastes like watered-down gruel, not a nourishing meal. It simply isn't serious enough. It's too playful and chatty and casual. Its joy just doesn't feel deep enough or heartbroken or well-rooted. The injustice and persecution and suffering and hellish realities in the world today are so many and so large and so close that I can't help but think that,

deep inside, people are longing for something weighty and massive and rooted and stable and eternal. So it seems to me that the trifling with silly little sketches and breezy welcome-to-the-den styles on Sunday morning are just out of touch with what matters in life.

Of course, it works. Sort of. Because, in the name of felt needs, it resonates with people's impulse to run from what is most serious and weighty and what makes them most human and what might open the depths of God to their souls. The design is noble. Silliness is a stepping-stone to substance. But it's an odd path. And evidence is not ample that many are willing to move beyond fun and simplicity. So the price of minimizing truth-based joy and maximizing atmosphere-based comfort is high. More and more, it seems to me, the end might be in view. I doubt that a religious ethos with such a feel of entertainment can really survive as Christian for too many more decades. Crises reveal the cracks.[18]

5. Our tone in preaching should be suffused with a *joyful confidence*. While we decry a smug and shallow triumphalism, we also have the confidence of being united to Christ, the eternal Son of God, the Firstborn from among the dead, the returning King! Neither injustice nor immorality, neither falling marital rates nor personal tragedies, neither natural disasters nor economic woes can stay God's hand or slow Christ's return one moment. Like the elderly John on Patmos, imprisoned on a tiny island by the mightiest of empires, so we speak to the powers of this age with no fear but rather with earnest warning, godly threats, and sincere desires for their repentance so that they may join us in the victory of the Lamb.

When It's Done

Few preachers who preach God's Word feel great when the sermon's done. I'm usually thinking about everything I didn't have time to say or even a few things I *did* say that I wished I *hadn't*. Then the time for the benediction slips up on me, I give it, and then I sneak to the back door to talk with people as they walk out. Sometimes people come to talk, and I'm humbled and encouraged by the ways they say the Lord used the sermon in their lives. Other times no one says much of anything, which bothers me more than I wish it did.

But the immediate feedback—as much as we crave the instant gratification—isn't the point. A pastorate is made up of a lot of sermons, and the fact is, most of those sermons are going to be singles rather than triples or home runs. But that's fine. If the Lord is so kind as to give you even a long string of singles, that's purely of His grace, and your congregation will benefit and grow from that. You score runs with a string of singles. So don't worry if you haven't hit a home run in a while—and if you hit one today, don't get cocky! Either way, go home, rest, thank God for the grace He gave you to teach and encourage His people again, take some time off, and then start the whole process over the next week. Our God is a good God, and week after week, sermon after sermon, He will give grace and strength and insight to the men who preach His Word.

[CHAPTER NINE]

Reviewing the Sermon

———◦◦◦———

What do you like to do on Sunday evenings after a long and
fruitful Lord's day with your congregation? Go to a movie
with friends? Get fast food and watch a TV show? Spend quality
time with your family? I (Mark) like all those things, too, but for the
last fifteen years, I've spent Sunday nights sitting in my study with
my staff, interns, and a few other friends talking about the day and
hearing critiques and encouragements.

Without a doubt, this weekly "service review" has been one of
the most helpful tools I have found for improving both our services
in general and my preaching in particular. Over about an hour and a
half, a dozen or so of us review every element of the day in turn, from
Sunday school classes to prayers to songs to the day's two sermons.
We think about how the songs flowed in the service and how well
the congregation sang them. We talk about how the service leader
did an excellent job welcoming visitors or how he failed to smile
through the entire service and lent it an unhelpfully melancholy air.

We talk about the prayers that were prayed and discuss how both their content and their heart came across in the context of the service as a whole.

And then, in the most detail and at the most length, we discuss the sermon, whether I preached it or someone else. Everything is on the table. We talk about the exegesis, the application, the introduction, and the conclusion. We talk about how the sermon affected our hearts, what challenged us, what we didn't understand, and what perhaps could have been done better, or wasn't done at all. Sometimes discussion ensues. Sometimes we all end up agreeing with one another. But regardless of how it goes, the regular discipline of inviting and receiving feedback on my sermons has been instrumental in my growth as a preacher. The men and women who give me feedback have shaped me over the years. They've taught me things about how people hear me that I might otherwise never have discovered. They've convinced me at times that I misunderstood some part of the passage I just preached. They've had good thoughts about the text that never crossed my mind. And, just as importantly, they've encouraged me to keep preaching, week after week, as they've explained how the text of Scripture, through my sermons, has challenged and encouraged them in the faith of Jesus Christ.

We would encourage you to adopt something similar in your own ministry. It doesn't have to look precisely like what we do at Capitol Hill Baptist Church. At Third Avenue Baptist, for instance, we don't do a service review on Sunday evenings. Instead, a few of us get together over coffee early on Tuesday mornings to talk through the prior Sunday. The important thing is that you open some lines of communication so that you can receive feedback on your sermons. That's not just so you can improve, either, as great a benefit as that might be; it's also a safeguard against error, a way for a few trusted members of your congregation to hold you accountable to do your job as a preacher well and not just mail it in week after week.

Occasionally people will ask us why we do a service review. We've already talked about some of those reasons, but we want to mention four more that we often give to people who ask. We do a service review in order to teach each other four important skills for any Christian minister: the ability to give godly criticism, to receive godly criticism, to give godly encouragement, and to receive godly encouragement. All those skills are tested in a profound way when you open yourself and your sermons up to being poked and prodded by certain trusted members of your congregation.

Giving Godly Criticism

Most Christians have no idea how to give godly criticism, how to correct and reprove in a way that is constructive rather than destructive. That's why negative feedback in our churches tends to come in a flood. People simply refrain from offering critical feedback at all because they think the whole idea is ungodly, and then when the situation becomes unbearable, it comes out in a flood of invective and frustration. Criticism, though, doesn't need to be like that. It is not inherently a negative thing. On the contrary, criticism is what the Lord uses to help us grow both as Christians and as preachers. And for that reason we need to take care to invite people to think critically and carefully about our sermons and then teach them to give us feedback on them in a godly way.

Think about Paul's words to Timothy in 2 Timothy 4:2. "Preach the word," he says. "Be ready in season and out of season; reprove, rebuke, and exhort, with complete patience and teaching." Two out of the three words he uses are unambiguously critical. They have to do with correcting error and setting an erring person on the correct path again. Proverbs 9:9 makes a similar point: "Give instruction to a wise man, and he will be still wiser; teach a righteous man, and he will increase in learning." Giving criticism in a godly way—and teaching and inviting others to do the same—is part of our job as pastors. But what does it mean to give criticism in a godly way? Several things come to mind.

First, any godly criticism will be given in the context of love, appreciation, and even encouragement. It's not often that *everything* a person has done is devoid of good. Almost always, there will be something to encourage before you move to things he did wrong or less than ideally, and you should take that opportunity. That doesn't mean you have to adhere slavishly to the old three-good-things-for-every-bad-thing ratio, but it does mean that your criticism shouldn't come out of nowhere. It should be given in a clear context of appreciation so that the person you're criticizing understands thoroughly that your criticism is coming from a heart of love.

Second, the criticisms you give should be *specific*. A general criticism that "I had a hard time following your sermon" is not nearly so useful to a man who's just preached as a criticism that "I had a hard time knowing where you were in your outline because you didn't flag the points sufficiently when you moved from one to another." Remember, the goal in giving godly criticism is to help the person you're critiquing to get better, and specific feedback can be implemented the next time that brother preaches in a way general feedback cannot.

Third, it's usually better not to give just a negative assessment of some part of a sermon but rather to give a positive alternative as well. For example, instead of saying, "You shouldn't have illustrated the point that way," it's usually better to say, "I understand the feeling you had that you needed to illustrate that point. I think you were right about that. But instead of doing it like you did, maybe you could have tried this." See the difference? The latter criticism gives a way forward. It provides a way for the guy being critiqued to think about how he might improve when he preaches again.

Finally, your criticisms should always be gentle even if they are firm. They should never be cutting or deliberately witty or calculated to make yourself look good. There's always a temptation to give criticism in a sharp or overly interesting way. And the reality is, that's easy to do. It's far easier to come up with a witty, biting criticism than to preach an entire sermon. So when you give criticism, do it gently even if firmly. Say that something was wrong or ill-advised as firmly as necessary, but don't do a rhetorical pirouette in the process. If you do, yes, you'll draw attention to yourself and make people laugh, but the reason for your critique in the first place—helping the preacher improve—will be lost. He'll simply stop listening to you.

Ultimately, that's the key to giving godly criticism: it's to keep always in mind the *purpose* of the criticism. Your goal is not to win approval for yourself or to prove that you would have done a better job than the preacher but simply to help the preacher do better next time. Keep that in mind, and your critique will be suffused with a gentle, firm, and ultimately edifying godliness.

Receiving Godly Criticism

If you're reading this book, then you likely find yourself on the receiving end of sermon criticism more often than you do the giving end. For some preachers, receiving criticism about their sermons is incredibly difficult. They find themselves getting defensive, or angry, or depressed if anyone has anything negative to say about their sermons. Being able to receive godly criticism, however, is a crucial means to a long, fruitful, and growing ministry. It's also a matter of wisdom. The book of Proverbs is full of sayings that press on us the importance of hearing words of reproof and correction. Proverbs 13:18, for example, tells us that "poverty and disgrace come to him who ignores instruction, but whoever heeds reproof is honored." Proverbs 15:32 says, "Whoever ignores instruction despises himself, but he who listens to reproof gains intelligence." Proverbs 12:1 puts it most forcefully: "Whoever loves discipline loves knowledge, but he who hates reproof is stupid."

Receiving criticism is never fun, but when it's given in a godly way, it's almost always beneficial. I (Greg) remember the first sermon I preached at Capitol Hill Baptist Church as one of Mark's interns. I also remember the service review that night; more than a decade later, what Mark said to me that evening has stuck with me. For one thing he made raucous fun of me for standing on my tiptoes through the whole sermon. I've tried to fix that problem for a decade now with nothing but failure as a result. He also told me, more importantly, that I should have realized that Jesus Himself interpreted the Old Testament passage I was preaching from and that I should have learned from Him how to understand it. At the time I didn't enjoy that criticism. I childishly wanted the sermon to be flawless. But looking back on it, that criticism of my sermon shaped profoundly the way I think about how to preach the Old Testament. If I want to understand it rightly, I need to look at how Jesus and the apostles understood it. I didn't know it at the time, but Mark was teaching me a profound lesson in the *regula fidei*, the principle that Scripture is its own best interpreter, and it's paid dividends for more than a decade now.

Most of us have a tendency to bristle when we hear criticism of our work. We tend to bristle and start thinking immediately of defenses against what the other person is saying. The key to receiving godly criticism, though, is to trust that the person critiquing your work really is doing so for your good, and then to work hard to see and understand what he or she is saying. Don't immediately defend or excuse; just listen and try to see what they saw. That doesn't mean you can never respond. When you review a sermon, everyone is learning, and sometimes the preacher's response to a particular criticism can teach everyone involved. But it does mean that you should receive the criticism and not immediately snap to a posture that rejects all criticism as illegitimate. Proverbs calls that "stupid." Don't do it.

And what should you do with the criticisms you receive? Well, you certainly shouldn't dwell on them to the point of discouragement. On the contrary, use them to grow! Use them to improve! Treat criticism like you would a bitter pill. Swallow it quickly and thoroughly, and let it do its work in your life and preaching. But don't feel a need to chew it up and savor it! Then, the next time you preach, remember the criticisms and put them to work. If you do, you'll "gain intelligence," as Proverbs says. And you'll become a better preacher as well.

Giving Godly Encouragement

Just as important as giving godly criticism is the ability to give godly encouragement. Believe it or not, encouragement is not always godly. There is a form of encouragement that is little different from flattery, and we ought to avoid that. We shouldn't, however, shy away from giving encouragement just because it can be sinfully corrupted. After all, every good thing can. In any review of a preacher's sermon, it's important not simply to give godly critique but also to give godly encouragement.

Perhaps the best way to do that is to give specific examples of how certain sections of the sermon—this application or that illustration—impacted your life and heart. Of course you should spend some time talking about the more technical aspects of the sermon— the main idea, the outline, the preacher's handling of the text, the way he used illustrations, whether he preached the gospel, and how he concluded. But if you want to give deep, lasting encouragement to a preacher, there really is no better way to do so than to recount how the Lord used his sermon to affect your life.

We're not talking here about flattery. Don't inflate your encouragement beyond the truth. Encourage where encouragement is due, criticize where criticism is due, and be silent otherwise. Similarly, be careful about overusing superlatives in your encouragement. If an illustration was good but not the best you've ever heard, say it was good, but don't say it was the best illustration you've ever heard. If you tend to use superlative words in every piece of encouragement you give, people will quickly realize that fact and learn to discount what you say. Save the superlatives for the superlatives.

Having a congregation that knows how to give godly encouragement can be a huge boon to those who preach the Word week in and week out. Preaching, by necessity, is an emotionally draining activity, and it is even more so if the only feedback the preacher ever receives is negative or even just silence. A congregation that knows how to encourage their pastor will spur him on, perhaps for decades, to keep preaching faithfully and powerfully.

Receiving Godly Encouragement

Most of us have no trouble at all receiving encouragement, at least not on the surface. Compared to receiving criticism, receiving encouragement is relatively easy. But of course it has its own dangers.

As we mentioned above, it's good when a congregation wants to encourage their pastor, to tell him how his sermons have affected their lives and point him to the fruits of his labor in the life of the church. And every pastor needs to hear that kind of encouragement. The danger, of course, is the heart's tendency to begin taking pride in that fruit. We look at the Lord's work in our churches and begin to mistake it for our own. To receive encouragement in a godly way is to receive it humbly with the recognition that any good fruit that comes from our preaching is God's work, the result of His Holy Spirit taking up our words and giving them power in people's lives.

We should stand in the pulpit every Sunday with a deep sense of dependence on God. We ought to know, deep in our hearts, that if He doesn't bless and empower our work, it will fail. When we see fruit, therefore, the praise is God's. When people are saved through our preaching, the praise is God's. When they repent of sin and awaken to a renewed love for Christ, the praise is God's. And we should be quick to give it to Him. The fact is, our ministry, just as much as our salvation, is a gift of God's grace. We aren't saved because we deserve it, and we don't stand in the pulpit every Sunday teaching God's people because we deserve it, either. We stand there because God has graciously blessed us with the privilege of doing so, and every bit of encouragement we receive should be accepted with a heart filled with gratitude to God.

So receive encouragement; don't deflect it. Don't insist that your people not give it to you. It is important and right that they should do so. Thank them for their encouragement, and take joy in it, but don't dwell on it to the point of self-confidence. With every bit of encouragement you receive, train your mind and heart to humbly acknowledge that all good things—your ministry, your ability to preach, His grace in allowing you to teach His people—are gifts from God above. And we who stand in the pulpit every Sunday to declare a message of grace should take particular care not to lose sight of that.

One Man's Experience of Service Review

Several times a year we invite a number of pastors and other church leaders to spend a weekend with us and participate in all the activities of our church, including the service review. Our hope is that they'll see in our staff and interns the spirit we've been talking about in this chapter, a spirit that graciously gives and receives godly criticism and humbly gives and receives godly encouragement. We also hope those men will see the benefit of doing something like this in their own churches. Here's a description of what one of those brothers saw when he attended our review of a Sunday he'd attended:

> If I were to summarize the meeting in a word, I would describe it as . . . detailed. The meeting progressed through every event of the day. They began by reviewing each of the Core Seminar (Sunday School) classes. Most of the classes had someone on staff in attendance. The service review leader (Mark Dever, this time) went through each of the classes and opened discussion concerning the quality of the lesson, the quality of the teaching, and anything that needed improvement (for example, one of the rooms had a noisy A/C unit running throughout the entire class).
>
> The group then began to review the Sunday morning service. Apparently, many of the leaders at Capitol Hill are educated in music. They spent a good deal of time reviewing not only the songs chosen, but also specific details of how the songs were played. . . . Another topic which was reviewed was the prayer. As I mentioned before, the morning service included a significant amount of prayer, and the prayers were led by different leaders in the church. This time of the review was spent critiquing each other's prayers. You may think this is sacrilege, but it seemed quite beneficial. One prayer was pointed out because of his abnormal use of high language during his prayer. It was recommended that he speak in a more conversational manner; "use contractions," Mark suggested. Another prayer was brought up because, due to a slip of the mind, something was prayed that was incorrect and unbiblical. At another point, the younger leaders asked the Senior Pastor for advice on how to prepare for leading

the corporate prayer. Overall, it seemed to be an uplifting review session.

Most of the review time was spent, unsurprisingly, critiquing Geoff's sermon. [Geoff was a pastoral assistant at CHBC at the time.] I was amazed by some of the detailed responses some of these men were able to offer. At one point, someone quoted an entire sentence from the sermon, verbatim. Although the details of the critiques are not terribly important to communicate here, it was very clear that the more experienced preachers had much to offer Geoff, who had considerably less pulpit experience, and that Geoff gratefully received the advice. . . .

Walking away from the service review, a few things stood out in my mind. First, the events of that Sunday were reviewed *in detail* by the church leaders. Surely, one reason so many people look to this church as a model is because of the deliberate nature of CHBC's leadership. Secondly, the critiques were given *and received* with humility. When an individual (especially the older ones) was critiquing someone else, the critique consistently began with praise before anything critical was brought up. Surely this made it easier to receive the critique. Everyone seemed to take critiques well, especially the more senior elders. Feathers were not ruffled and morale was not reduced by anyone's comments. Creating and maintaining a leadership culture which can accept criticism humbly surely requires much effort—and is definitely worth it.[19]

We agree, and we pray the Lord will help us do that for our good as preachers, for our good as Christians, and for our churches' good as they grow in Christ through the preached Word of God.

[PART THREE]

Sermon Transcripts

Introduction

In this third part of the book are two sermon transcripts, one from Mark and one from Greg. The point of these is not to show off any particular skill at preaching but rather to give you an idea of what it might look like for us to review each other's sermons, to talk about them and give each other feedback. Interspersed through the transcripts are notes on a conversation Mark and Greg had with one another about the sermon. Criticisms as well as encouragements are noted, as are any explanations or further comments the preacher might have wanted to make about a particular section.

Because we wanted to show you what a review of actual sermons might look like, these transcripts are only lightly edited. The content of the sermons hasn't been changed from the day they were preached, and nothing substantive has been added or corrected. Sentences have only been edited when they simply didn't make sense in written form, for the purpose of making the sermons readable and understandable without recourse to the audio. These aren't particularly the best or the worst of our sermons, either. They are just sermons we have preached recently. We wanted you to see our sermons, in the rawest form possible—the good, the bad, and the ugly.

We're not holding these sermons out as models of everything we've talked about and advocated in this book. At times we hit the nail on the head; at other times we probably missed it entirely. But hopefully seeing these transcripts—and the comments we made to each other about the sermons—will help you see how the principles we've argued in this book play out in our own preaching ministries.

The first sermon, by Greg, is entitled "You Meant It for Evil, but God. . . ." An exposition of a full fourteen chapters of Genesis, preached in December 2010, it is a treatment of the life of Joseph. The second, by Mark, is entitled "Jesus Was Forsaken by His Father." Preached in April 2011, it is an exposition of the apostle Mark's account of Jesus' death on the cross. Both of these sermons, we hope, will be not just instructive but even edifying for you as you read them.

"You Meant It for Evil, but God . . ."

Genesis 37–50

December 5, 2010

Greg Gilbert

Coincidences are funny things, aren't they? They just kind of happen, and they surprise us, and sometimes we find some amusement in them, and sometimes even some amazement.

Let me tell you about one coincidence. It's kind of a coincidence writ large in the life of myself and my wife. Some of you are going to know this already because we tell it with some glee and also some foreboding. But I want you to recognize this about me and my wife and maybe especially about our offspring.

My wife's middle name is Booth. That's because a grandfather of hers had the last name Booth. And he was descended from a particularly famous Booth in American history. Anybody know which

Booth I am talking about? The first two names were John Wilkes—the man who assassinated Abraham Lincoln.

My mother's maiden name is Surratt. Anybody know the significance of Surratt? A few weeks after John Wilkes Booth was killed by the authorities after he assassinated Abraham Lincoln, an accomplice of his was hanged in Washington for helping him to pull off this plot against the president. Her name? Mary Surratt. Yes, I am descended from Mary, and my dear wife is descended from John Wilkes Booth. So that means the two lines of one of the greatest assassination plots in American history have now come together in my three little children! I'm sure the Secret Service has an eye on them every single minute of every single day!

MARK: Was this sermon part of a series?

GREG: Yes, on the whole book of Genesis.

MARK: Oh. Well, that makes a difference. You didn't say that. It would have been good to say so. People who are just walking into your church without knowing what's going on will wonder. Just saying where you are in the series will help people who just pop in.

MARK: You have a good intro here, but it could have been better.

GREG: I know, I know. It was kind of throwaway. It was cheap, wasn't it?

MARK: No! I just think it could have been better. You know how?

GREG: How?

MARK: By saying that you met Moriah right here in D.C., just a few blocks from where Abraham Lincoln was assassinated and Mary Surratt was hanged.

GREG: (Laughs)

MARK: She was hanged just a few blocks from here, you know? Right where the Supreme Court sits now.

GREG: I didn't know that. I thought it was over in Virginia.

MARK: If you had your Ph.D., you'd have known that.

GREG: (Laughs) Oh, that's how it's going to be, huh?

MARK: Anyway, good introduction. It would pull people in.

GREG: You do heavier stuff in introductions—philosophical and theological stuff.

MARK: Sometimes. Yea, usually. But the accessibility and knowability in this one is very good. It will appeal to a lot of people, where mine can be narrower.

GREG: I try to use intros, like you say, as a funnel, to bring people in. But I'm doing it more for attention than for ideas, I think.

MARK: I thought you did it well. Now, what you didn't do, by doing that kind of intro, you didn't remove any objections. Often what I'm trying to do is to set up my foil in a sympathetic way so that their defenses go down. So what some guys try to do with humor, I try to do with understanding. I try to bring defenses down so that they know the guy up there has heard their concerns and understands them, feels the weight and pull of them.

GREG: Yea, you do front-load applications, but you tend to front-load appeal to non-Christians more than just about anything.

MARK: Yea, I do.

MARK: On your manner—you were clear, you were loud, you spoke quickly. You had good energy . . .

GREG: Wait, wait. Spoke *too* quickly or *good* quickly?

MARK: Good quickly. A friend told me one time after he heard me preach for the first time—he came up and said, "I bet people tell you that you talk too fast, don't they? That's not true. That's got good energy in it; that's why people sit on the edge of their seats listening to you because you have so much energy when you speak, and speed is part of that."

GREG: So do people tell you a lot that, even though your sermons are an hour, they don't feel like it?

MARK: Yea, all the time.

GREG: Me, too, at least sometimes. And I think that has something to do with speed of speaking.

Coincidence. It just kind of happens. Well, we are looking this morning at a story, beginning in chapter 37 of Genesis, that is absolutely chock-full of coincidences—or at least that's how this story is often talked about. It is a well-known and a well-loved story. You've got this local boy who started out as a shepherd up in Canaan who becomes the second-in-command of one of the most powerful nations on the planet. At least that is how it is usually understood—a

rags-to-riches story. Local boy made big. That's the way people typi-
cally talk about this story of Joseph becoming the vizier of Egypt.

But actually, if you read the story rightly, if you understand the
way it plays out in Scripture, you understand that it is not just a
mere rags-to-riches story, and we are not just supposed to feel good
because the local boy has made it big. Actually, the story that we are
going to be looking at today from Genesis is the story of the amazing
power and sovereignty of God worked out in the stuff of human life.
And it leads us not just to feel good for Joseph, this mistreated little
boy who becomes a king, but to rejoice and to marvel at God and His
amazing sovereignty over the whole thing.

Well, turn if you will to Genesis 37. We are going to be looking
at everything from chapter 37 all the way to the end of the book this
morning because the whole thing is really one long story about the
life of Joseph. We are not going to read the whole thing, obviously,
but let me give you a run-through of the entire story before we notice
some things about it.

Most of you are going to know the contours of the story of
Joseph pretty well. Chapter 37 opens with Joseph having a series of
dreams in which his family bows down to him and, because he is a
young boy and he doesn't understand how this is going to affect his
brothers, he runs to them after he has seen them all bowing down
to him and he says, "Guess what I dreamed. I dreamed that all of
you and mom and dad are going to be bowing down to me one day."
Well, his brothers, of course, the other eleven are incensed at him,
and they decide they're going to kill him.

Well, things happen and they eventually just throw him in a pit
and decide that instead of killing him—because they don't want the
blood on their hands and because they can actually make a profit off
of the kid—they sell him to a group of traders who are headed south
towards Egypt. They arrive at a price, hand Joseph over to these traders, and off he goes to the South towards Egypt.

Well, arriving in Egypt, Joseph is then bought by the captain of Pharaoh's guard, a man named Potiphar, and in time, because God blesses Joseph in his service to Potiphar, Potiphar winds up putting him in charge of the entire house. So he works in Potiphar's house, having great success, until the day when Potiphar's wife begins to try to get Joseph to sin with her. During one of those times when she is trying to get him to sin, she grabs his cloak and Joseph flees the house. She, of course, blames the whole situation on Joseph. She takes no responsibility for the sin herself but says to her husband Potiphar, "It was Joseph who did this. And look, I have the proof right here in his cloak. " Well, Potiphar, not knowing the truth, throws Joseph in jail.

Soon afterwards, two other officials—Pharaoh's chief baker and his chief cupbearer—are thrown into prison with him, and within a few days both of them have dreams. And they don't know how to interpret those dreams. So they are telling Joseph one day about these dreams, and Joseph says, "Well, I can interpret those dreams for you. And really, it's not me who is doing the interpreting anyway; it's God. It's the Lord who can interpret those dreams. But let me tell you what your dreams mean. They actually mean sort of the same thing, although they come to different ends. Both of you," Joseph says to them, "are going to have your heads lifted up. For you, Mr. Chief Cupbearer, to have your head lifted up means that you are going to be restored to your position. You are going to be serving Pharaoh again. Everything is going to go well for you. But you, Mr. Baker, your head is going to be lifted up, too, but in a slightly different way. Your head is going to be lifted *off* because Pharaoh is going to execute you and hang you from a tree."

Well, three days later on Pharaoh's birthday, it all happens exactly as Joseph says. The chief cupbearer to Pharaoh is restored to his position, and he begins serving Pharaoh again. The chief baker is executed, and the cupbearer forgets all about Joseph and leaves him in the prison where Potiphar had put him.

Two years pass by, and Pharaoh eventually has a sleepless night in which he has two dreams that he can't interpret. Well, the chief cupbearer who has been in Pharaoh's service now for the last two years remembers that, "Oh, there was this fellow in prison who was able, with God's help, to interpret my dreams. And actually, it turned out exactly like this guy said. So why don't we call him up from prison and have him, O great Pharaoh, interpret the two dreams that you had on this sleepless night."

So they call Joseph up from the prison. Pharaoh tells him the dreams, and Joseph interprets them for him. He says, "Those are the same dreams. They have different forms, but they mean exactly the same thing. There are going to be seven years of amazing abundance in Egypt. You are going to have more food than you know what to do with. And then following those seven years, there are going to be seven years of great famine, and the people of Egypt are going to starve unless you appoint a man over the resources of the Empire to gather grain into the cities and put it into silos and hold onto food so that you can make it through those seven years of famine." Well, Pharaoh is amazed both by Joseph's interpretation of the dream and by this plan that he has for making it through the seven years. And so he appoints him to be what is called the vizier of Egypt, which means that the only difference between Pharaoh and Joseph the vizier is the throne itself. Joseph had all of the authority in Egypt, but he just didn't have the royal title or the royal throne.

So Joseph begins this work of taking food from the people and storing it up in the cities during the seven years of abundance so that they will have plenty of food for the seven years of famine. Well, when the famine comes, Joseph's brothers up in Canaan, who sold him into slavery in the first place, are told by their father to go down to Egypt because they've heard, even way up in Canaan, that Egypt has food because of what Joseph has been doing in his work of storing it up. So Joseph's brothers come down to Egypt. And they meet this man who is over the whole thing, but they don't recognize him as Joseph. Joseph recognizes them, but they don't recognize him.

Well, Joseph sells them some grain, but in the process he grabs one of the brothers, Simeon, and says he is going to hang on to Simeon until the other brothers go back and get their youngest brother Benjamin and bring him back to Egypt because Joseph wants to see his younger brother Benjamin. They are the only two that were born of both Jacob and Rachel, if you remember, so he wants to see his full brother. So he sends them back to Canaan.

The brothers get back to Canaan, and they tell Jacob what this man—this vizier of Egypt—said. "He kept our brother Simeon," they say, "but he wants us to bring Benjamin back, and then he will sell us some more grain and let us go." Jacob says no for a time, but eventually they run out of food, and so Jacob says, "OK, you can take Benjamin back to Egypt and show him to this man. Then you can get some more grain and bring it back to Canaan again." So they show up in Egypt one more time with Benjamin in tow, and Joseph sees Benjamin and is overwhelmed by seeing his brother. So he invites all of these brothers to dinner.

Well, he decides to test them to see if they are still as hateful and as selfish as they were with him. And so clandestinely and secretly, he takes a silver goblet from his own table, and he has it put in Benjamin's sack as he sends them back towards Canaan. A few hours later, though, Joseph says to his own men, his own soldiers, "I want you to chase them down and catch them and see if there is anything in their sacks."

So the men chase down the brothers as they are headed back to Canaan, and they begin to search the sacks. And one of the brothers says to the men who are chasing them down, "Look, we haven't stolen anything from you. And if you can find anything in any one of our sacks, that man is going to become a slave to you. We will give him up." But of course, they search the sacks, and what do they find? Well, they find the silver goblet in Benjamin's sack. So they all turn around again and head back to Egypt, and Joseph tells them, "I am keeping Benjamin as a slave."

Well, one of the brothers, Judah, had already told his father when they were headed back to Egypt, "Look, I will put myself up as security for Benjamin. And if I don't bring Benjamin back to you, you can give me the blame for it for the rest of my life." So when the vizier says he's going to keep Benjamin as his slave, Judah steps up and realizes what that means for him. So he says to the vizier, "O high and mighty lord, let me tell you what I told my father. I told my father that if I don't bring Benjamin back, then he can blame me for the rest of my life."

Joseph the great vizier is overcome with emotion. He sees now that Judah has changed, that he is willing now to give himself in the place of Benjamin, to stay on as the vizier's slave and let Benjamin go home to his father. He sees something going on in Judah's life, and he breaks down and weeps and reveals himself to his brothers. He says, "I am Joseph. I am the one you sold into slavery. And this is what the Lord has done with me."

Well, after that Joseph calls the whole family down to Egypt, and they weather the famine. Joseph takes food from the people and then sells it back to them, and they all weather the famine. The end of the story then is Jacob blessing Joseph's own two sons, Ephraim and Manasseh; and then he blesses his own twelve sons before he dies. When Jacob dies, there in chapter 50, Joseph takes an entourage from Egypt to bury his father, and then he lives sixty more years in Egypt and dies. Then the last line of the book says that he is embalmed and put in a coffin in Egypt.

MARK: You ran through the Joseph story at the beginning and took ten minutes to do that. I don't know that you needed to take that long. It's a pretty well-known story, and you're going to rehash it when you're getting into it in the rest of the sermon, anyway. So I thought that could have been a little shorter.

GREG: You know, that was just two short paragraphs in my notes. It wasn't very long at all. I just said more than I had written down!

MARK: Yea, I know how that goes.

GREG: You stick really close to your manuscript, don't you?

MARK: On and off.

GREG: Because your manuscripts are 13 pages, aren't they?

MARK: 9 to 13.

GREG: Mine are 4. 3 to 4. What do you think that says?

MARK: I think that says you're confident and you repeat yourself a lot.

GREG: (Laughs) OK. Are you saying I did that a lot here? Repeat myself a lot?

MARK: No you didn't.

GREG: Ooooohhh.

So that is the story told quickly. It is actually a long and engaging story. I hope you had time to read it this past week before you came. But here is the main idea, I think, of this story of Joseph and his rise to kingship in Egypt. The main idea, I think, the thing that this passage is striving over and over and over from beginning to end to teach us, is that we ought to marvel at God's power and rest in His sovereignty. We are to marvel at God's power and rest in His sovereignty.

Now, as we talk more about this story, I want us to focus really on three things from it—three different points from the story, and therefore three points to this particular sermon: (1) God's absolute sovereignty, (2) Joseph's quiet trust, and then (3) Joseph's surprising irrelevance. (You will have to hang with me for that one. I saw a bunch of heads pop up when I said that. Yeah, I didn't say relevance, I said irrelevance!) So God's absolute sovereignty, Joseph's quiet trust, and then Joseph's surprising irrelevance.

> MARK: You had three points to the sermon, and you made them very clear. At a conference a few weeks ago, a friend criticized me for having such an artless sermon on Psalm 4. By artless, he meant that I made the skeleton of the sermon very clear, with the points right out there. He said he works very hard to cover over the skeleton so nobody notices it, so it's hard to take notes on and it's just a seamless narrative that pulls people along.

> GREG: Wow. Yea, I tell guys *not* to do that.

> MARK: So you're of the knobby-knees school of preaching?

> GREG: Yea! I think it gives people handles. Otherwise I think you have a smooth surface, and there's nothing to grab on to.

> MARK: I agree. I also think it makes it easier for people to listen longer, because it gives them mile markers, so they know where they are.

> GREG: Yep. Though in my sermons the first point is typically *hugely* longer than the others. I think that's just my own fault.

MARK: Well, in this sermon the first point was *hugely* longer than the others.

GREG: Yea, that's typical.

MARK: That's what I've heard. . . . It was twenty minutes long. . . . I thought the outline was good, by the way, those three points.

So the first point of the sermon: The first thing that I think this text is laboring to tell us is about God's absolute sovereignty. If there is anything in this story that stands as the main theme, it is the fact that every step of the story, every tiny, seemingly insignificant event is happening at God's direction. He is meticulously superintending every single one of these events to bring about a certain outcome, a specific outcome that He wants to happen.

That, in fact, is the reason that Joseph has these dreams in chapter 37. He has these dreams of the sheaves of wheat in the field bowing down to the sheaf that he has gathered, and then he has another dream that the sun and the moon and eleven stars are bowing down to him. And the point of it is that God has an intention to make that happen, to have Joseph's family bowing down to him eventually.

Now, if this was just a rags-to-riches story, if all this were just a story of a local boy made good, then the dreams don't serve any purpose whatsoever. In fact, they are kind of anticlimactic. I mean, can you imagine if you were watching a movie that Hollywood had put together, and at the very beginning of the movie they tell you the whole ending? There is no twist at the end. There is no nothing. Here in the first two minutes of the movie, they just throw the last twenty minutes of the movie in right at the beginning. It just kind of ruins it.

My wife and I walked in on a movie once. We thought we were going into the correct theater and we sat down. We knew we were a little bit late, but we thought we were like two minutes late. So we sit down in this movie, and things are happening, and we were thinking, "Wow, this seems to be solving a lot of problems right at the beginning." Well, it turns out that we had walked into the wrong theater. And then the credits rolled and we were just completely flummoxed because we have just seen the last fifteen minutes of the movie. Well, we went and found the right theater, but you can see how it ruins the story. If this is a rags-to-riches story, there is no point in these dreams. But if this story is not meant to make us marvel and feel good for Joseph, but if the story is meant to teach us—and maybe especially even to teach Joseph and his brothers—that God is absolutely sovereign over every detail, that He is moving us forward to a certain conclusion, then the dreams are crucial. It is God calling His shot. He is telling you in advance what He is going to do, and the glory comes to Him because the dreams come true. That's why the dreams are there.

> MARK: I thought this illustration of you and Moriah walk-
> ing into the movie late was good.

This is also what Joseph meant with that great summary statement in chapter 50 verse 20. Turn over there because it's kind of the goal of the whole thing; everything here in this story is laboring to get to chapter 50 verse 20. This is the point of the story. Joseph's brothers in chapter 50 verse 15 are scared. Their father is dead, and they think the only thing that has been keeping Joseph from killing them is that their father wouldn't like it very much if he did. So they send Joseph a letter and actually lie to him there in verses 16 through 18. They say, "Look, it was dad who said you really should forgive us when this is over with. So if you love your father, don't kill us."

> MARK: And I thought your pointing to Genesis 50:20 was
> theologically correct.

Well, Joseph just kind of throws that away. Look in verse 19 at what he says: "Do not fear, for am I in the place of God?" And then verse 20: "As for you, you meant evil against me, but God meant it for good, to bring it about that many people should be kept alive, as they are today."

Now look carefully at the wording of that statement. "As for you, you *meant* evil against me, but God *meant* it for good." You see that? God *meant* it for good. It's not that He *used* it for good; it's not that He *turned* it for good. It's not that God took lemons that He wasn't expecting and made good lemonade out of it. It's that He *meant* all of this to take place. He meant it. You see that? God meant for Joseph's family—He meant for His chosen people—to be finally in Egypt, and so therefore He meant for Joseph to be in a position as the vizier of Egypt to bring the family to Egypt. And so therefore He meant for Joseph to go to Egypt in the first place. So even as these brothers are trying to be rid of him, even as they are trying to do evil, even as they are trying to put a stop to these dreams and make sure that these dreams never happen, they are actually doing exactly what God meant for them to do so that He could bring about what He wanted to happen.

You can see God's meticulous sovereignty here in every detail of the story. You can see God's sovereignty in the fact that they decided on a whim not to kill him because they are scared of having blood on their hands. You can see it in the fact that the first caravan that passed by is headed south to Egypt and not north, and they decide to sell him. You can see it in the fact that out of all of the millions in Egypt, Joseph is sold to Potiphar, the man who is in charge of a really high-ranking prison where high officials of Pharaoh would likely be. You can see it in the lies of Potiphar's wife that landed him in prison. You can see it in the dreams that the cupbearer and the baker had.

You know what the point was of the dreams of the cupbearer and the baker? It's not that God was all that interested in telling those particular guys what was going to happen to them in the future. That's not why God was doing that. He was doing that so that the cupbearer would remember that Joseph is able to do this when Pharaoh had his dreams. Even with Pharaoh's dreams, the point wasn't so much to warn Pharaoh about the coming famine. That's not the point. The point is not so much to make it so that Pharaoh takes the right actions to save the people of Egypt from the famine. God let a lot of other nations *not* store up food for the famine. The point is that God wanted the cupbearer to remember that Joseph could interpret dreams, and He wanted Pharaoh to hear that, and He wanted Pharaoh to call Joseph, and He wanted Joseph to interpret the dream, and He wanted Pharaoh to put Joseph in a position of power so that He could bring the family back. In meticulous detail it was all being directed by the hand of God.

> **MARK:** I thought it was fun going with you through all the details of God's meticulous sovereignty.

Now that raises a question, doesn't it? "Really? Seriously, are you saying that God is sovereign over everything, even the simple action of the brothers selling their brother Joseph into slavery to a bunch of Midianite traders who were headed to Egypt? You are really saying God is sovereign even over that?"

That's an important question, isn't it? Because there's some part of us, as we think about this, that thinks, "You know, I wonder if it would actually be better to think that some things are outside of God's control. And wouldn't it make Him a morally better God if He weren't sovereign over everything? Wouldn't it make it easier for me to believe in Him if I could point to certain things that are happening and say, 'No, God was as surprised by that as I was? No, God didn't have a hand in that? God is not sovereign over that. He was surprised and saddened by that. He is not sovereign over that.' Wouldn't that be better?" Well, this passage is actually one of the most important ones in the Bible for thinking through questions like this—God's sovereignty and how it relates to our own experience of making real, genuine choices and having responsibility for those choices.

There are two things I think that we need to learn from this. There are two things that we need to see very clearly from this story and that we have to hold together as both being true. So we have to do a little bit of theology here and think through what the Bible says and what the book of Genesis is telling us about God's sovereignty over these events. So let me give you two statements that you really should understand to be absolutely true, and yet you are not going to be able to see how they exactly fit together.

First of all, God is indeed sovereign over the brothers' actions. He just is. It all comes about by God's direction. And Joseph has no doubt about that whatsoever. We have already seen in chapter 50 verse 20 where he says, "You meant it for evil, but God meant it for good." And then also a little bit earlier in 45:5–7, when he is talking to his brothers, he says, "God sent me here." And then in verse 8 he even goes so far as to say, "It was not you who sent me here; it was God." See, Joseph knows from the very bottom of his being that God is indeed sovereign over his brothers' action of selling him. That is the first statement.

The second statement is that Joseph's brothers are fully responsible for their actions. The fact that God ordained those actions from the beginning and caused them to happen the way He meant for them to happen doesn't change the fact of the brothers' responsibility. The Bible holds them responsible for it over and over and over. Chapter 37 verse 11 says that they were jealous. Chapter 37 verses 4–5 and 8 say that they hated Joseph. And then one of the main themes that runs through the story—you see it popping up all over the place—is that the brothers themselves recognize their guilt. They know they are guilty, and they are scared to death about it. So when the money shows up back in their sacks and they open up the sacks and see the money, they think, "Oh my goodness, God is out to get us!" Now that is not a normal reaction to finding a sack of money! But that is what they thought because they had a guilty conscience; they knew that what they did was wrong. They knew that they were responsible for it, and they thought God was beginning finally to punish them.

> MARK: And then the two lessons about God's sovereignty and human responsibility were just good basic teaching. You did a really good job, I thought, of just walking through the immorality of their actions—how the Scriptures ascribe morality to their actions, how there's a moral weight ascribed to them.

> GREG: And the fear that they feel in the story points to their guilt!

> MARK: Yep, that's right.

So those are the two statements. God is sovereign over the brothers' actions, and Joseph's brothers are fully responsible for their actions. Now I realize that it is hard to put those two things together. But you see these two truths being borne out all over the Bible. So in Exodus for instance, God says at the beginning of that story that He is going to harden Pharaoh's heart. "I will harden his heart, so that he will not let the people go" (Exod. 4:21). And then the text tells us over and over again that "Pharaoh hardened his heart" (Exod. 8:32).

In 2 Samuel the Bible says that the Lord incited David to take a census of the people as a means of bringing judgment on the people. And then after the census is done, David says, "I have sinned greatly." You see, God incited him to bring about a certain end, but David recognizes his responsibility. "I have sinned greatly." You see? Nothing, not one thing in these stories, not one thing in the world or in the universe, is outside of God's sovereignty. And yet we as humans are fully responsible for what we do.

We read a little bit earlier in the service from Acts 4, and you see that this is true even of the greatest act of evil that has ever happened in the history of humankind—the crucifixion of Jesus. I don't know if you caught it in that Scripture reading, but think again about Acts 4:27 in particular, where the believers pray this: "In this city there were gathered together against your holy servant Jesus, whom you anointed, both Herod and Pontius Pilate, along with the Gentiles and the peoples of Israel." You see what they are saying there: They were gathered together against Your anointed. They gathered, they were against Him, they crucified Him, and they are responsible for that and guilty of it. But you know what the next phrase says? They "were gathered together against your holy servant Jesus, . . . to do whatever your hand and your plan had predestined to take place" (v. 28). They are responsible and yet God is sovereign.

> MARK: Always good to go to Acts 4:27 to show divine sovereignty and human responsibility.

Now what do we do with that? We know these two things are true. We know that they are both taught in Scripture, but what do we do with them? Why do they matter? What do we do with our hearts in the face of something like this, something that maybe we can't even understand?

Well, for one thing we humble ourselves. We humble ourselves and we stand still. We stand in awe of a God like this who is sovereign over every atom in the universe. Not one thing moves apart from His sovereignty and His ordination. "Be still," God says, "and know that I am God."

So often we have a tendency as human beings to think that if two things don't make sense to us right now in this particular moment, then therefore they can't make sense ever to anyone, and therefore they are just nonsensical. Do you ever notice that? Do you ever notice that when you are presented with two different things—maybe it's

God's sovereignty and human responsibility, maybe it's something else—and if your mind can't put the two things together right now, you just throw up your hands and pronounce judgment on the universe and say, "Well, then, it can't be! It's absurd!" Do you ever notice that? Well, friend, let me just encourage you to have a little humility and recognize that your mind is finite and God's mind is infinite. And so it's entirely possible that there is something in God's infinite mind that just won't fit in your finite mind. Humble yourself and be still and know that He is God.

Yes, there is a tension between human responsibility and God's sovereignty. We know there is a tension there. We feel that tension. But for us to simply declare that it is nonsensical or that one of these statements must be not true and that we have to figure out a way to throw one of them away, is to say that our minds must be as big as God's. And that is simply not the case. Now, I'm not saying that we should not think about this. No, certainly not; of course we think about it. We look at Scripture, we do theology, and we think. There's plenty I could say here, actually, about all kinds of things like "concurrence" and "asymmetrical ordination" and "libertarian versus compatibilist free will." If we had a couple of hours, I could talk through those things with you, and we could actually make some headway in seeing how these two truths almost intersect. But at the end of the day—even as we think through all of those really interesting and really helpful theological categories—at the end of the day, we come to the point where we just have to bow on our knees and say, "I am not God. And He has not given to me to see how those two lines intersect." So we humble ourselves.

Another thing we do is that we rest in God's sovereignty. We rest in the fact that nothing happens in this world that is outside His control. Not one atom sheds an electron apart from God's sovereignty and ordination. Friends, there is no comfort, there is no rest in thinking that certain things that happen to us in this life are outside of

God's control. There is no comfort in that. When something comes against you, when there is evil that is being perpetrated against you—whether it's human evil or just the circumstances of life—there is no comfort in thinking that that is outside God's control. Because if it is, then where are you going to turn? Who do you cry out to for help? The comfort comes in knowing that nothing happens to you but that which is from the hand of God who loves you. That is where the comfort comes. And so we rest in God's sovereignty.

Finally, we just stand in awe of God's sovereignty and His majesty and His power. We stand in awe of it. There are moments where you just stand in hushed silence before power like that. You see and you recognize and you acknowledge the crown of the universe on God's head, and you bow your knee and you bow your face and you say, "God, You alone are worthy." Oh, but then brothers and sisters, there are the moments when you rise to your feet and you recognize and you rejoice in the fact that the brow that crown sits on is smiling down at you because you are one of that King's children! Do you understand the power of that? Do you understand the power that God has? And then do you understand the fact that the one who rules over everything is also the God who gave His life to save you? The God who holds the scepter of the entire universe in His hand is the God who stretched that hand out so that a nail could go through it because of His love for you. Paul writes in Romans, "If God is for us, who can be against us?" (8:31). The answer? Nothing and no one because the Lord of the universe is the Lord who loves you and is working all things together for your good. It's an amazing thought.

> MARK: Now I'll tell you what I thought was the most confusing point of your sermon. You began to apply this point of "God's absolute sovereignty" with this section about humbling ourselves, resting in God's sovereignty, and then standing in awe of it.

GREG: Yep.

MARK: But I found myself wondering, "Whoa whoa whoa. Did I just miss him beginning point 2? Because point 2 is "Joseph's quiet trust." It's his response to God's sovereignty. So I thought it was messy having those points here instead of . . .

GREG: Right, because those *are* the second point. Yea, good point.

MARK: The reflections themselves are excellent. All three are superb responses to God's sovereignty.

GREG: So would it be OK, do you think—if the second point *is* the application of the first point—just to move into it and *not* apply the first point?

MARK: Correct. That's correct. It'd be far less confusing.

GREG: OK.

God's absolute sovereignty. That is the first point.

Second, Joseph's quiet trust. Joseph's quiet trust. You see that in him through the whole story. From the time he has these dreams and through everything his brothers and Potiphar put him through, Joseph seems to have this remarkable confidence in the fact that God is sovereign over everything that is happening. And it's not obvious to him all the time what is going to happen. What is he thinking when he's down in that pit and his brothers are up at the top having dinner together and trying to figure out whether they're going to sell him or kill him? And then they drag him up out of the pit, and they start negotiating with these Midianite traders, and they put him in the wagon and send him off south? He must be thinking, "I am never going to see my father again." See, Joseph doesn't know the end of the story like we do, and yet throughout the story he remains quietly trustful of God.

Joseph goes to prison and languishes there for two years. This is not a meteoric rise to the top of Egypt. It is not that Joseph is carried along by this wonderful train of angels that is just pushing him forward until he arrives and, wow, he is the king! No, he spends *two years* languishing in prison, thinking that God has forgotten him. But he never loses faith in God. Even in the midst of all of that, he serves Potiphar well and heartily. He serves well and heartily in the jail even. He doesn't lose his integrity with Potiphar's wife, and he takes care to let the cupbearer and the baker and even Pharaoh himself know that the interpretation of the dreams isn't coming from him; it's coming from God. He remains faithful to God throughout.

I think Joseph, in this quiet trust of God even in the midst of these unbelievable circumstances, is a good model for us as Christians. For one thing, one of the ways Joseph is a good model is that you, like Joseph, need to decide right here and right now that you will trust and obey God regardless of your circumstances. You need to decide right here and right now that you are going to trust God regardless of your circumstances and you are going to obey God regardless of your circumstances. Even when you look around your life over the years and you don't see any blessing whatsoever, yet you remain faithful to God.

How easy, how tempting would it have been for Joseph to look around and find himself in Egypt and think, "Dreams schmeams! None of that happened, did it? My brothers were supposed to be bowing down to me, and now here I am, a thousand miles away in some Egyptian dude's house serving him. I quit!" And then perhaps he'd just embrace the whole Egyptian life. How easy would it have been for him to do that? Or sitting in the prison, how easy would it have been for Joseph to just say, "I am done with this—this faith in God stuff, all these promises that God said He is giving me. I have been sitting here for two years, and what have you done? Nothing. I am still here."

Friends, it would be easy for you to do that, too, at certain points of your life. "God, I have been waiting on You. I have been trying to be patient. I have been keeping on a good face, and I have been saying nice things about you for years. And look where it's gotten me. I am still right here where I was five years ago." Or, "God, I have been struggling with this sin for years. I have been praying my heart out for You to take this temptation away from me. And what have you done? Nothing."

Brothers and sisters, hold on. Hold on. Keep struggling, keep waiting, keep obeying and trusting God. Listen, God's providence is a long road. Sometimes God's providence is even longer than the lives we lead. Do you realize that? There are a lot of Christians who struggle and fight and wait their entire lives, and they *die* struggling and waiting and fighting. They never get what it is that they want so desperately. Think about all of the Israelites that lived and died in slavery over those four hundred years in Egypt—waiting, calling out to God for redemption, and it didn't come. And they died. And the last prayer off their lips was "God, redeem us from slavery." And they died.

God's providence is a long road. And yet even when He decides not to give us what we so desperately want, we believe Him and we love Him and we trust Him. It's like Peter said: "Lord, you have the words of life. Where else are we going to go?"

And that leads us to something else, I think, too. You, like Joseph, need to learn to be joyful and serve well where God has put you. Learn to be joyful and serve well where God has put you. Do you think Joseph was thrilled to be in Potiphar's house? He had a nice place, to be sure. But do you think Joseph was thrilled to be there? Really, when his family is in Canaan and he loves his father? It's obvious when he sees them again. What does he do? He breaks down in tears. So obviously everything wasn't well in Joseph's soul. He wasn't thrilled to be in Potiphar's house. He wasn't even thrilled to be vizier. He breaks down when he sees his father and his brothers. But he served well. He served well in Potiphar's house. He served well in Potiphar's prison. He served well as the vizier of Egypt.

The truth is that none of us as Christians should ever be entirely content with where we are right now in this life. We shouldn't be content with it because we are looking forward to another city that God built. We are looking forward to being with Christ, and we are not there yet, and so there is always going to be some seed of discontent in our hearts as we wait. And yet we are called to serve well right here. Wherever God has you, you are called to serve well and heartily. Don't mail it in. Don't mail it in with your job; don't mail it in with your church. Don't mail it in with anything that God has given you because this is where God has you for now. Don't just do half-baked stuff because you think, "Well, I don't want to be here anyway. I didn't ask for this job. This isn't what I wanted to be doing. I want to be over there doing that. And God is going to take me there someday." Well, maybe He will, but maybe He won't. And for now God has you where you are, and He expects you to serve as if you are serving Him. This is where God has you. And whether He intends you to rise and be a king or to live out every last one of your days as a servant in Potiphar's prison, this is where He wants you for now. So you serve your King well, and you serve your King joyfully with a quiet trust exactly where He has you. That's what Joseph did, and that's what we should do.

MARK: Your point 2 was only eight minutes long. But that's because about ten minutes of it were sitting in your point 1.

GREG: Oops.

MARK: But you applied this wonderfully to the Christian waiting patiently on the Lord. The pastoral high point of the sermon was no doubt where you were calling for people to trust in God, to not be impatient with Him. That was where you sounded your most passionate. I have no doubt it's where you felt your most passionate, and I have no doubt you got the most comments on that point. So (Gives a thumbs-up) . . . put that in the book.

GREG: (Laughs) I'll put it in brackets.

So that is the second point. Joseph's quiet trust.

Number 3, the third point of the sermon: Joseph's surprising irrelevance. Now hang with me because that is slightly overstated. Obviously I don't mean that phrase, surprising irrelevance, in any absolute sense. Joseph is obviously a key link in the story. The story explains how Israel wound up enslaved in Egypt at the beginning of Exodus, so it is a key link, and he is not irrelevant in that sense. But I want to show you something that is a little bit striking after this whole story. Genesis, as we have been studying it over the last few weeks, is really the story of God's promise to Abraham and how those promises get worked out in the lives of Isaac and Jacob and Joseph, right? That's the story. That's the structure of the book of Genesis. Abraham, Isaac and Jacob and Joseph. Abraham, Isaac, Jacob, Joseph. That is the story of Genesis. In fact, Joseph has the longest story of any of them, right? Fourteen chapters in Genesis. He is the only guy among them that winds up being a king. Abraham, Isaac, Jacob, Joseph.

Now turn to Matthew 1 because I want to show you something really striking. It is the genealogy of Jesus, which is where all of this has been headed anyway. All of the promises to Abraham—we have been talking about him for weeks—they are all headed to Jesus ultimately. Abraham, Isaac, Jacob, Joseph. Abraham, Isaac, Jacob,

Joseph. Look at Matthew 1:2–3: "Abraham was the father of Isaac, and Isaac the father of Jacob, and Jacob the father of *Judah* and his brothers, and Judah the father of Perez and Zerah."

No Joseph. He doesn't even show up. Fourteen chapters of Genesis, rises to be the second in command of all of Egypt, but he is skipped and ignored here. He is surprisingly irrelevant when it really, really matters.

I think that is just another reminder to us of God's sovereignty. In fact, the whole story of the twelve sons of Jacob is one massive, beautiful, mixed-up canvas on which God paints the words, "You did not choose me but I chose you." At every turn in the story, the question is, "OK, the promises started with Abraham, went to Isaac, went to Jacob. Jacob has these twelve sons. Now, to which one of those twelve sons are the promises going to fall now?" It's just one massive, mixed-up story, and what we would expect to happen, over and over again, *doesn't happen*. And what we would *never* expect to happen *winds up happening*.

> MARK: Your third and shortest point, "Joseph's surprising irrelevance," was a wonderful point. Very fun to turn to Matthew 1. Extremely well done—very encouraging, biblically correct. "God doesn't want your trust to be in a plan, but in Him"—that's how I'd shorten and sharpen what you said. . .
>
> GREG: (Laughs)

Who is going to bear the promises? And then for chapters and chapters of Genesis, it is like a shell game among them. It's like one big game of Kill the Carrier. The promises fall to this one guy, and then something comes and smears him and he loses the ball, and then they fall to another one and he takes off running and he gets smeared, too. And you are just wondering, "Where are the promises going to land?"

You start out thinking, "Well, it must be the firstborn, that's Reuben." Then you find out in chapter 35 that OK, it's not Reuben. Reuben sins and gets rejected. So it's not the firstborn. OK, well, what about the second and third born, Simeon and Levi? Oh, no, both of them, they wind up sinning also and are rejected. Well, OK, what about the fourth born, Judah? And you think, "Well, maybe." One, two, and three are gone, so now we're down to the fourth, and you read along in the story a little bit and you are thinking, "Yea, maybe Judah. Judah is doing okay." Doh, but then there is chapter 38. Maybe not Judah. OK, so what about the favorite son, Joseph? Yeah, that's the ticket! It's Joseph. I mean, look. We've got fourteen chapters about Joseph, and he has this coat of many colors, a very royal look-ing thing. And then oh, there he goes! Look, there he goes! All of a sudden, he is king of Egypt, and you think, "Yeah, that's gotta be it! The promises are falling to Joseph." And then you get to chapter 49 of Genesis, and you find out—wonder of wonders!—it's not Joseph. It is Judah, the fourth born. The one who sinned.

Look at chapter 49 verses 8–10. This is Jacob blessing all of his sons, and, shockingly, this is what he says to Judah: "Judah, your brothers shall praise you; your hand shall be on the neck of your enemies; your father's sons will bow down before you. Judah is a lion's cub; from the prey, my son, you have gone up. He stooped down; he crouched as a lion and as a lioness. Who dares rouse him? The scepter shall not depart from Judah nor the ruler's staff from beneath his feet until tribute comes to him; and to him shall be the obedience of the peoples."

See, all the sons are there, right? All twelve of them are there, and they are being blessed. And there is Joseph at the end of the line, number eleven, dressed in his kingly robes from Egypt. And every-body around him is thinking, "Yes, we will bow to Joseph." Jacob blesses Reuben, Simeon, and Levi, and everyone expects him to pass over Judah just the same, and yet he says, "Judah, the scepter will not depart from your feet until it comes to the one for whom it's been waiting, Jesus Christ."

See, God is sovereign. He does what He wants. You can't read God's providence forward. You read it backward. Don't ever, ever say, "This is what God has in store for me," or, "This is what He does not have in store for me." The reality is you just don't know. And you know why you don't know? You don't know because God doesn't want your trust to be in some inviolable life plan that He e-mails to you. He wants your trust, through thick and thin, through good and bad, to be in Him. You hang onto Him for dear life.

There is one other thing that I think we should notice here, just in conclusion. It's the fact that in letting these promises fall to Judah, God shows Judah enormous grace—the same Judah whose idea it was to sell Joseph into slavery in the first place, the same Judah who embarrassed himself in some other ways in the story, too. It is this Judah between whose feet is the scepter that Jesus Himself will take up when He comes.

Even though Joseph isn't finally in the ancestral line of Jesus, I think he shows us even here in Genesis a brilliant picture of Jesus in one particular way. He forgives his brothers. After all they have done to him, they are scared to death. If you read through the story, they are scared to death that Joseph is going to take revenge on them and kill them for what they did to him. Even after their father dies, as we saw, they are scared of him. And yet the whole time Joseph knows their sin, and yet he wants nothing more than to forgive them.

Friends, Jesus is the same way. I think so many times people think, "I have done this, and I have done that, and I am convicted of my sin. But how can I go to Jesus in the condition I am in now? He would just take it out on me. He would just take revenge on me. He would reject me, and I would deserve it." No friends, Jesus is more like Joseph than that. Even as you are stewing in fear, even as you are finding all kinds of reasons to walk away from Jesus,

Jesus is standing there with open arms, ready to lavish life on you just like Joseph did to his family.

You realize, don't you, that Jesus died for sinners just like you? And if you come to Him in faith, renouncing those sins and saying, "I don't want those anymore. I want You, and I need You to save me," He stands with life in His hands, ready to give it to you. That is ultimately the message of Genesis—God's mercy, God's grace to people who didn't deserve it, to people who were swindlers, to people who were liars, to people who were impure in all kinds of different ways, and yet God pours out His grace.

In other words, He pours out His grace on people just like us. Let's pray.

> MARK: Great point about God's grace to Judah, and also about Joseph showing grace to his brothers. I thought your second-highest point, pastorally, was "I can't go to Jesus; He'd just take it out on me." You just caught the sinner well there, and the excuses Satan whispers in his ear to misunderstand and misrepresent Christ. So that was just excellent there. Just a superb sermon, and you should preach this again and again. Though you could probably shorten the first thirty minutes of it down to twenty or fifteen.

"Jesus Was Forsaken by His Father"

———— ◦⊙◦ ————

Mark 15:16–41

April 10, 2011

Mark Dever

Christianity is, without doubt, the oddest of all the religions in the world. If it doesn't seem that way to us here in Washington, D.C. in the twenty-first century, it could only be because of the centuries and millennia of familiarity that we have with it. They have dulled us to its strangeness.

Confucius died at age seventy-two or seventy-three, respected, even revered. The family line of Confucius is, in fact, still known. It is the longest extant pedigree in the world today. The eightieth lineal descendant of Confucius was born in Taipei on January 1, 2006. The details of Gautama the Buddha's life are more obscure, but it seems that he died respected and revered—even celebrated—in his eighties, surrounded by his disciples. Mohammed died at age sixty-three in

Medina, with his head being cradled in the lap of Aisha, the favorite of his thirteen wives. Buddha, Confucius, Mohammed—all of them died as old men in the midst of communities which respected and even revered them.

And then there's Jesus. Jesus' ministry could hardly have ended more differently. Jesus' three-year ministry concluded by Him being executed. Jesus' brow was not crowned with the slowly advancing graces of old age. He was not surrounded at the end with admiring disciples. Those He had most poured Himself into had either betrayed Him or denied Him or deserted Him. Those who surrounded Him on that last day were soldiers who struck Him, and criminals, and passersby, and even priests who mocked and insulted Him. Those regarded as wise considered Him a dangerous fool. He was charged with being at least a confusing, disrespectful teacher and at worst a threatening revolutionary.

So as we considered last week, Jesus' earthly ministry would be concluded by His being killed, and that not in the heroic way of Socrates, calmly drinking hemlock, surrounded by admiring, awed, grieving students but rather in a public, painful, humiliating, and degrading way.

This is so surprising to many people who first look into Christianity. They expect that all religion is basically the same, even if you have these different packages put on them as they're made in the religion factory. And they assume that Christianity is really just like all the other religions, except that it has a Jesus wrapper on it. Yes, it has some things that are distinctive to Christians and Jesus—different symbols, different songs—but the ideas are basically the same.

But friends, when you begin to consider it seriously, that idea quickly falls away. If you're here today and you're not a Christian, and you've been talking to your Christian friend like that, I just want to inform you here and now that you're just showing that you don't know anything about what you're talking about. I don't mean to insult you, but it's just the case. You're showing that you believe television. You're showing that you believe popular media. You're showing that you've never done any careful research yourself, not even a cursory reading of the documents of different religions—and certainly not the New Testament.

Jesus did not die in old age and prosperity, in respect and renown. He was not wealthy. He was not universally respected. He didn't have His best life now. He was not beloved by one and all. He was executed, and it was an execution that was religious and political. He was executed like criminals were. In fact, He was executed with criminals, as a criminal.

Jesus' death came quickly and violently. It was a public, deliberate rejection. It was a punishment that, in one sense, was the deepest point of injustice ever enacted in the long and dark annals of human injustice. And yet this was not mere injustice. There was, behind and beneath the human injustice, a rightness that makes the cross today a symbol of goodness and love and righteousness and even mercy.

> GREG: This was a great, typically Deverian introduction, pulling in non-Christians, pulling in people who might not be very interested in Christianity, but also beginning to set the hook on why Christianity is different from other world religions. I thought that was very good. Two things about the intro, though: Did you have a particularly heavy service that led up to this? From word one your voice and demeanor were extremely heavy.
>
> MARK: I think you've just forgotten what it's like at CHBC.
>
> GREG: Cause they're all heavy, you mean?
>
> MARK: Yep. And yes, that service was pretty heavy.

GREG: Well, this was a heavier than average introduction for you, I thought. But then again, what are you going to do? Are you going to stand up and start making jokes when your text is "My God, my God, why have you forsaken me?"

MARK: Many would, I fear.

GREG: True. Well, I think the heaviness was right in this case. But it does make the point again that it's important to key your service to the text you're going to be preaching and not let them be independent of each other.

GREG: You had kind of a surprising thing here. The first time you addressed non-Christians directly, you *whacked* them. You said, "You're just showing that you don't know anything about what you're talking about." Do you often insult people like that?

MARK: I do. It's a gift I think. (Laughs)

GREG: What are you thinking there?

MARK: Look, they've chosen to come here. Yea, I clearly just did that on the fly. It wasn't in the notes. I was just ticked off. Evangelism through chiding—this is why I'm not a megachurch pastor!

GREG: (Laughs) Well, it was a little striking.

MARK: I justify chiding from the Old Testament prophets.

GREG: OK, Jeremiah. Moving along.

How could that be? How could something so scandalous become so beloved? Well, to find that out, we want to turn to Mark's Gospel in the New Testament. We're in chapter 15 of Mark, beginning at verse 16. It's found on page 1009 in the Bibles provided, and you will be helped today if you follow along. If you're not used to listening to sermons or not used to listening to sermons here at Capitol Hill Baptist Church, we study the Bible. We think the Bible is God's Word, so we open it up, and we leave it open for an hour, and we look at it, and we think about it together.

When I refer to chapters, they're the large numbers, and verses are the smaller numbers after them. We're in chapter 15, and we're beginning with verse 16. (Read Mark 15:16–41.)

> GREG: How often do you explain what chapters and verses are, and does that bug your congregation?

> MARK: Two out of three sermons, probably—and no, the congregation appreciates it. At least the ones who speak to me about it do.

> GREG: Why do long-time Christians appreciate that?

> MARK: Because they know that I'm being helpful to those who are visiting and who don't usually read Bibles, and it's good for them to listen with those ears.

> GREG: And it makes them feel comfortable, probably, bringing neighbors and relatives and friends.

> MARK: Exactly. And it might make them wonder if they even *know* anybody who wouldn't know their way around a Bible. Maybe it will convict them, too.

Friends, the heart of our passage is right there in verse 37. "And Jesus uttered a loud cry and breathed his last." He gave over His spirit. He released it. Jesus died. This strange and riveting fact, more than any other, separates Christianity from other religions. For us who are Christians, Jesus' death defines us, so much so that the means of His execution, the cross, the symbol of His weakest moment and His deepest humiliation, is taken by the whole world to be our logo.

The Divine Son of God took on flesh and lived a truly, fully human life, never ceasing to be divine, living in true fellowship with His heavenly Father, depending on His Word, doing His will. And this embodiment of God, of humans made in God's own image, was . . . killed? What's going on here? How can we make sense of this? We want to consider Jesus' end today and understand it.

What we are considering this morning is applicable to every area of our lives. It is the basis for all of human conduct. Were I to start doing applications in this sermon, I could just read you 1 Peter 2, or I could read you Philippians 2. I could read you the whole book of Hebrews. This is where Christianity is generated from. So what we're going to do, unusually this morning, is this: Exactly because this is at the center of everything, I want to spend our time today staring straight at this passage, especially at the death of Christ, and giving all of our time to understanding it. That's because by understanding more of Jesus' death, we will understand Jesus, and we may even understand ourselves.

This is my prayer for you today.

What do we see in this passage? We'll spend the longest time just working through our first point, and then we'll briefly notice some more aspects of the significance of Jesus' death we see here.

GREG: Let's talk a little more about a lack of balance in sermons. You knew, right at the beginning, that your first point was going to be longer than the others. And it was *massively* longer. Of these four points, "the horror of sin" was much longer than any of the others. Why was that? Is it OK to have an unbalanced sermon? If so, when?

MARK: Well, points 2, 3, and 4 were all about the solution to the problem. But especially here, it's the problem itself—the assumption of sin—that feels very alien to people today, at least expressed in this kind of stark language of Scripture. Anytime you think you're going to have to do some of that kind of basic explaining, you might end up with unbalanced points.

GREG: Yea, and of course sometimes the text just kind of demands it. One thing I've noticed in preaching is that a lot of difficult theological stuff is often packed into the first part of Scripture passages, and then it's just a matter of working those things out. But a lot of the heavy lifting has to be done in the beginning. That can lead to some imbalance, too, that's not really your fault.

First, we see the horror of sin. Jesus' suffering and death here is really the culmination of our sinful human rebellion against God. What was started at the Garden of Eden is worked up to a fever pitch here. What is it John 1:10 says? "He was in the world and the world was made through him, yet the world did not know him, and his own people did not receive him."

Is that not a gruesomely perfect picture of this rejection? Soldiers with the approval of legitimate human authority mock Jesus, and they beat Him and finally crucify Him. We see here in verse 16, "The Roman soldiers led Jesus away from Pilate, the Roman governor who had just condemned Jesus to death." They led Him to the Praetorium, the governor's residence there in Jerusalem, probably in the fortress Antonia. Even in His being led we see something of the humility that marked Jesus' whole life. From that first day to the last, from His humility and being born in the manger to now here, being led around by this company of soldiers, the Lord Jesus humbled Himself.

At the Praetorium the soldiers perform a mock coronation of this King of the Jews, as Jesus had been derisively called. Look at verse 17: "They put a purple robe on him, then twisted together a crown of thorns and set it on him. And they began to call out to him, 'Hail, king of the Jews'" (NIV). They didn't miss anything, did they? Deriding Jesus' authority by putting a purple robe on Him, some silly costume version of what a king would wear, the soldiers mocked Him, and you see that their mocking turned cruel as they twisted together a crown of thorns and set it on Him.

"In the beginning was the Word, and the Word was with God, and the Word was God. . . . In him was life, and that life was the light of men. . . . He came to that which was his own, but his own did not receive him. . . . The word became flesh and made his dwelling among us. . . . We have seen his glory, the glory of the One and Only, who came from the Father, full of grace and truth." And when this one came, this one who was the most majestic of all who were ever in the human race, how was He received? How was He recognized? With this fake robe and this painful crown, and the cruel mocking submission, "Hail, king of the Jews. Hail, king of the Jews (John 1:1, 4, 11, 14).

Friends, do you see that our sin is so deep that we can speak the truth and still be blind to it? You understand something of the nature of sin from this. It's almost certainly the case that the most serious sins in our own lives we're barely even aware of, so blinding is sin by its nature. That's why we join a local church. That's why we hear God's Word preached. That's why we regularly pray and return to God's Word.

But these soldiers didn't only speak derisively of Jesus. Their rejection of Him was violent. Look at verse 19: "They struck him." It's the kind of beating Jesus had just endured before the Sanhedrin up in chapter 14. It sounds strikingly like the parable Jesus had just told back in chapter 12 about how the tenants would receive the owner's servant and finally the owner's son. That prophetic parable, which they were so upset about when Jesus told it just a few days earlier, they are now fulfilling before their very eyes, as these soldiers strike Jesus.

And don't forget to notice where they struck Him. They struck Him on the head, as if just to make clear that their crowning of that head was done only in mocking derision. They hit Jesus' head. They wanted it understood clearly and pointedly that they owed Him no respect. And they didn't do it just once. You see that at the beginning of verse 19. They did it again and again. They didn't just hit Jesus. They beat Him.

What a picture this is of our opposition to God, our violent, repeated rebellion. Friend, in a spiritual sense, hasn't this been you? Those of you who are Christians here this morning know that's the case with us. We have repeatedly opposed God when He has been completely clear with us. That clarity alone has not secured our love or our obedience, but we have chosen again and again to obey ourselves, our own whims and desires, regardless of what God, our Maker and Judge, tells us.

And friend, if you're here not as a Christian, I think I may have offended you by telling you that this is a picture of you. But it is. This is what the Bible says of all people, that we have, all of us, decided to reject God. Do you wonder why there's trouble and strife in this world? Well, you can point to all the physical challenges there are. You can point to natural disaster. But friends, even within human society, the Bible tells us why. The Bible tells us that we were all made in God's image, and so we are all of value and worth. So there's no person whom a Christian should not value and care for. So frankly, we will defend you and your rights no matter what religion you are; in fact, we want to encourage you to enjoy the goodness of God in this creation and beyond. But the Bible also tells us that there is something wrong with all of us, that though we are made in the image of God, we have all rebelled against Him.

And so this historical event is not just a parable. This really happened. It also depicts and illustrates what we have all done in our rejection of God. Even so, the horror of this sin is not yet fully appreciated here if we don't notice, there in verse 19, the mocking, sarcastic homage these soldiers paid to Jesus. They mocked out hymns to Him. They bowed in pretend prayer and praise. They spat on Jesus. These mortal, passing creatures who should have praised Jesus instead showed the most base, disgusting disrespect for Him.

Friends, in all of this we see something of the ugliness of sin. This is what sin is. It is disobedience to God, our rejection of His authority in our lives. It is a disregard for Him, and even more a positive personal rejection of Him. The point of this is not the physical suffering. Do you realize how restrained Mark is in his depiction here? He doesn't dwell on the gory details, and there were gory details aplenty. The point is the personal rejection of Jesus.

> GREG: I thought the first point of the sermon, "the horror of sin," was wonderful. You unpacked the text in a way that left you feeling extremely heavy by the middle of it. You talk about the kinds of people who are rejecting Jesus and the various ways they were rejecting Him. So by the middle of that point, it seemed like the congregation would have been silent. Again, were you going for that kind of heaviness?

> MARK: Yea, yea. I want them to realize that the rejection of Jesus was complete. If we're reaching here the absolute fever-pitch of humanity's rejection of God, I wanted them to feel the enormity of it.

Friends, you can see a spectacle on a film, which can concentrate on all the gory details. But if they're not explaining to you with words the significance of the death of Jesus, why He died and what that has to do with us, they're missing it entirely. The Gospels tell us *why* Jesus died. The Gospels explain it to us.

GREG: Why did you take a shot at the movie *The Passion*?

MARK: That wasn't in my notes. It was gratuitous.

GREG: Yea, but it made an important point.

MARK: Yea. I think that it has been God's way with us, ever since we lost sight of Him in the garden, to do great things that we can see—the exodus, the incarnation, the crucifixion and resurrection—but to use words to explain those signs and symbols. He doesn't just give us mute actions; He explains the actions with words. That's what I was trying to poke at in that movie. I think that movie tugged at people's emotions, but I fear it allows people to bring their own meaning to the events and import their own meaning into it and take that as if that's the point or the thrust of what God was doing in Christ rather than what He was actually doing—which is explained in the text of Scripture.

There's a very interesting verse over in James 2. Let's turn there for just a moment because I want to illustrate something about the nature of sin. Sometimes Christians will hear Psalm 51, "Against thee, thee only have I sinned" (v. 41 KJV) and they'll think, "Really? Sin is just against God? I sin against other people. Why are you telling me sin is just against God?"

Well, it's because, at its root, that's what sin is. It is a personal opposition to God. Look here in James 2:11. James is explaining the importance of loving your neighbor and not breaking the law, and he says in verse 10, "For whoever keeps the whole law and yet stumbles at just one point is guilty of breaking all of it" (NIV). Now why, if you just break one law, are you said to be guilty of breaking all of it?

Now the illustration preachers often use is that it's like a chain, so that if you break one link in the chain then the whole chain is broken. That's true, but I think it misses the point of sin. Look why James says that if we break one sin we've broken them all. Look at verse 11. "For he who said, 'do not commit adultery,' also said, 'do not murder'" (James 2:11 NIV). The hinge is in who said it. Both these commands, separate as they are, come from the same person, from God. The point of sin is that we are disobeying Him. It is a personal rejection of His authority in our lives.

> GREG: OK, I'm going to give you some of your own medicine here. You had a section in the first point where you talked about James 2, how breaking one law is actually breaking the whole law because it comes from God's mouth. I thought that point unfortunately lifted the feeling of heaviness, to ask everyone to go to another section of Scripture. I think it's a great point, obviously; I just thought probably you could have done it without breaking the good sense of heaviness you'd cultivated. Maybe do it in the second point about substitution, and that would help even the points out a little bit, too.

> MARK: What I was trying to do was biblically illustrate the personal rejection of Jesus, to point out that sin is the personal rejection of God. That's why I put it there.

> GREG: Yea. Did you think about doing that without having the church turn there? Just make the point without going there?

> MARK: Yea, that could very well have been a better idea.

So going back to the Gospels and to Mark 15, what we see here in these soldiers' mocking of Jesus is simply a scarily clear, sharp picture of what all sin is by its nature. It is a personal rejection of God.

Mockery like this, using even the wit and humor of God's image in us to deride God, only puts us under His good and right condemnation and in need of His grace, yet having absolutely no claim on His grace. We have not showed ourselves to be loving creatures, careful of our Maker, careful of His plans and designs for us.

Well, the soldiers ended this mock coronation. Perhaps it was the press of time. They wanted to get this over and done with that day if they could. Generally the Romans left the upright beams of the cross in the ground. They were too heavy, and it would be impractical to move them. The person being crucified would carry the crossbeam, often about one hundred pounds or so. But Jesus was likely weakened from the beating He'd just endured, not to mention the night of no sleep.

And so we see here in verse 21 that these soldiers conscripted Simon. They get to the place outside the city walls, the place called The Skull, where executions were done. It was a prominent location by a major road going into the city. This was part of the purpose of crucifixions, after all, to make sure that everyone could see and that everyone would know and understand what happened to those who dared to rebel. And so there they prepared to crucify Jesus.

Now it is just at this point that I suggest to you that any good story—certainly any good story from antiquity—should have had the hero saved. If this were just a story we were looking at, if this were something meant to make us feel warm toward Jesus and identify with Him, we'd expect Him to be saved. Crucifixion occurred in stories from antiquity. It was as much a part of some ancient adventures and romance stories as the guillotine was in stories from revolutionary France.

But in those stories the hero is always freed. Only the evil ever really suffer this fate of crucifixion—grave robbers, people who killed their husbands or wives, and hardened criminals. But the hero of the story always, *always* escapes just before the threatened and unjust crucifixion. Crucifixion simply represented the supreme threat, the tension that was screwed up to the highest pitch, and then his friends would come in and save him. That's how stories go.

So this is what we might expect, then, as Jesus is brought through the crowd that day, with Simon carrying the cross. Then suddenly His disciples, recovered from their cowardice, newly organized, perhaps with shiny swords and fast horses, break through the crowd and apprehend the unjustly deserted, condemned, beaten, and forsaken Jesus, and whisk Him away to freedom and recovery, thus securing for Him a place in the people's memory for ages to come as a heroic figure in romantic myth.

Friend, if you're here and you're not a Christian, if you knew the first century better, you would know that if this were just a story, that's the story that would be written. That's what will make people engage with the protagonists and believe, "Yes, yes, hero. The hero wins in the end. Follow His teaching." Crucifixion was the greatest shame that culture could inflict. But that kind of escape is not what happened because this is no mere story. This is history. Instead, we have this grotesque conclusion that would have horrified any reader—Jew, Roman, Greek—who picked this up and began to read it, expecting to sympathize with Jesus.

There in verse 23 they offered Him wine mixed with myrrh. Perhaps it was a sedative offered as a kindness before they drove the nails in. Perhaps it was offered to produce more pain. Whatever the reason, it fulfilled Psalm 69:21, and Jesus rejected it. And then in verse 24, Mark records, with his typical clipped style, these shocking words: "They crucified him."

Friend, if you come back tonight, we're going to look at one of the most amazing pieces of Scripture in the entire Old Testament—Psalm 22. We won't take time to read it all now, but in Psalm 22, written a thousand years before Christ, King David wrote in Psalm 22:16, "They have pierced my hands and my feet. I can count all my bones. People stare and gloat over me. They divided my garments among them and cast lots for my clothing." I remember when I first read that verse as a young Christian. I think I had a New Living Bible paraphrase, and I was sitting in the Madisonville Public Library. When I read it, I was so sure there was a misprint in my Bible that I called our pastor at First Baptist Church in Madisonville. I called him to try to explain to him, "Hey, I have a Bible here with a misprint in it. I mean, surely this is from the New Testament, and somehow they've sold this to me with this actually here in the Old Testament." Friend, read Psalm 22 this afternoon. See what happens in God's Word. See how prophecy is fulfilled in the most amazing ways.

The soldiers put up the formal charges against Jesus. He was crucified because He claimed to be the King of the Jews, so His rising form on the cross should be a good dissuasive to any would-be rebels or terrorists who were coming up to Jerusalem that day.

And Jesus' crucifixion seemed to confirm the religious leaders' rejection of Him because they knew, from the law of Moses in Deuteronomy 21, that anyone who is hung on a tree is under God's curse, and they assumed that the one thing the Messiah would never be is cursed.

The soldiers could divide up Jesus' clothes because they had stripped Him naked. The cross was for shame and humiliation as well as pain and execution. Jesus, in His poverty, had nothing left on earth, literally. Suspended naked between heaven and earth, He was a priest who carried no sacrifice with Him to the altar. *He* was the sacrifice that day.

> GREG: I love how you pay attention to the details in the text. The one that stuck out was how they first crowned Jesus' head and then hit Him on the head, just to underscore that this crowning is not real, and it speaks to your willingness to sit and stare at the text for a long time.

MARK: Yea. One thing about that, the fruit of meditation. I was talking to a brother recently who was preaching on the story of the Pharisee and the tax collector, from Luke 18, and I told him, "You know, your great task in preaching this, I think, is to imagine how people would have heard it when Jesus first told it. And one thing they would do that's different from the way we'll normally react, is that they're going to assume the Pharisee is a really good guy. So if you just make him an evil figure—a clear and obvious hypocrite—and let the tax collector be basically a good guy, I think you're going to reinforce people's self-righteousness. What you're going to have to do to make the point Jesus had in mind here, I think, is make that Pharisee really sympathetic to us. So we should present him as a champion of justice, as a sincere and good man. I think when we understand that, then we'll begin to feel the weight of this story better. That's the kind of thing we can begin to see through just meditating on the text."

But lest we think that all this sin is somehow only reflective of that subset of humanity hardened in war, skilled in violence and death, like these soldiers, Mark makes it very clear in verses 27–32 that everyone, from robbers to ordained ministers, refused Jesus and rejected Him. Maybe we're not as surprised at the cruelty of the Gentile soldiers, but even from His own nation Jesus was not afforded anything but hatred and scorn.

I'm not sure who in this parade of mockery in verses 27–31 are the most surprising participants. Perhaps it was the robbers. I mean, the fact that they were being executed suggests they were more than just thieves. They probably had just participated in an uprising. Just as Isaiah had foretold, Jesus was numbered with the transgressors. This was no band of brothers, no fellowship of friends. In verse 32 we see that even those who were crucified with Jesus heaped insults on Him. "Save yourself and us," one of them said to Jesus, almost as if to say, "Shut up. I hate You for what You're teaching, that You can save anyone when I am here dying like this. If You are not going to get me out of this mess right now—*this* problem—I don't care what You have to say."

Friends, they didn't just insult Him once, but they kept doing it. It was a reviling and an insulting that continued on. Even this is a picture of human sin, isn't it? Even when we are condemned and guilty, when we know that we have been wrong in some ways, we still find it in ourselves to judge other people, to condemn others, to notice and magnify others' faults. And Jesus was willing to endure even this twist of human humiliation for us.

But were their actions more shameful than those of the religious leaders there in verses 31 and 32? We really wouldn't expect anything different from those whom even the surrounding culture disdains. We understand criminals acting like that. But the religious leaders and the Bible teachers—surely they would not participate in mocking the very one they claimed to worship. But then, if you've been following along in Mark's Gospel, you know that we've seen the truth of that verse in John, "His own didn't receive him." So here, in their spiritual blindness, they too mock.

In more of the deep irony that marks the Gospels, in these sarcastic shouts, these chief priests and teachers of the law become some of the first evangelists. "He saved others but He can't save Himself." That's true, isn't it? He would save others, and He could only do that by not saving Himself. Jesus taught that even the Son of Man did not come to be served but to serve and to give His life as a ransom for many. Friends, if Jesus was to save others, He could not save Himself. It was just as Isaiah prophesized: "We considered him stricken by God, smitten by him and afflicted" (Isa. 53:4 KJV). Who should know all these prophesies better than these teachers? And yet they rejected the Messiah. They who should have worshipped and led in worship instead rejected and mocked their own King.

Verses 31–32, "In the same way the chief priest and the teachers of the law mocked him among themselves. 'He saved others,' they said, 'but he can't save himself. Let this Christ, this King of Israel, come down now from the cross, that we may see and believe'" (NIV). But of course they would not believe. It was like Jesus had taught earlier; they would not be convinced even if someone rose from the dead.

Mere religion is no guarantee of spiritual understanding or virtuous living. Lots of people can be religious. You can be Christian religious, Buddhist religious, all kinds of religious. Religion alone won't save anyone. In the rejection of Jesus here, we are witnessing the pinnacle of man's revolt against God. The rebellion, begun in the garden, engulfs all of human life. We see that prisoners are sinners; but so, too, are priests. Jails and churches have a lot in common, and one of the most important things we share is that we are sinners all. None of us has escaped the ravages of sin, criminals or Bible teachers. We have all been willing rebels against God and against His authority in our lives, and Jesus gave us the clearest opportunity to express it. Can you see it here?

In verses 29 and 30, we see that even the casual observers who had nothing at stake; those who were just walking by, probably going into the city in the morning, even they hurled insults at Jesus as they strolled past, mockingly calling out to Him to save Himself, and misquoting His teaching to Him. Look there at verses 29–30: "Those who passed by hurled insults at him, shaking their heads and saying, 'So: You are going to destroy the temple and build it in three days, come down from the cross and save yourself!'" (NIV).

And friends, again, it's just as with last week. The more you know the Bible, the more you see all the prophesies swirling around and coming to fulfillment. It's as if these people were *trying* to fulfill these prophesies, these people who probably had no idea of them. Psalm 22:7–8: "All who see me, mock me; they hurl insults, shaking their heads. 'He trusts in the LORD; let the LORD rescue him. Let him deliver him since he delights in him'" (NIV).

Even casual comments can reveal significant thoughts, can't they? So extensive is the human rejection of God that even casual passersby have to get in their two cents' worth. It's as if they would not want it thought that human sin is only the preserve of public criminals or religious hypocrites. It's as if they're jealous to make it known that, "No, no, no. Everybody sins." Behold the wide variety of ways that the incarnate God is opposed, the various forms and shapes our sin takes. Our sin is horrible, and it appears nowhere more horribly than here.

As terrible as our sin was, however, there was something still worse and better to come. That was all number one: we see the horror of sin.

Number two, we see in Christ's death here the cost of substitution. You see, in His death Jesus bore God's punishment.

Look again at verse 34: "And at the ninth hour"—that's 3:00 in the afternoon; the Romans calculated from 6:00 in the morning, so the third hour is going to be 9:00, sixth hour is noon, and the ninth hour is 3:00 in the afternoon. "At the ninth hour Jesus cried out in a loud voice, *'Eloi, Eloi, lama sabachthani?'* which means, 'My God, my God, why have you forsaken me?'" (NIV). This is the verse we'll be thinking about from Psalm 22 tonight, if you would like to end your Lord's day with some more meditation on this.

I think I'm safe in saying here that we are on the holiest ground in all of Scripture. We are in the relationship of God the Father with God the Son, and we must think and speak very carefully if we are to understand this correctly. God the Father is here forsaking Jesus, not in the sense of forgetting Him or ignoring Him, and certainly not in the sense of hating Him. Rather, God the Father is punishing

His Son, treating Him as if He had committed all the sin that He was bearing. Jesus had accepted this cup. This is why He came. Jesus cried out in anguish because He bore His Father's punishment.

Now, whether we come here as aged Christians or longtime non-Christians, understanding Christ's death as a substitute is fundamental to understanding the very heart of Christian hope. This is God's plan. "In Him," the Bible says, "we have redemption through his blood, the forgiveness of sins, in accordance with the riches of God's grace that he lavished on us with all wisdom and understanding" (Eph. 1:7–8 NIV).

I want us to briefly consider three questions: Why a substitute was needed, how a substitute could be, and why a substitute was given.

First, then, why a substitute was needed. The Bible is clear in teaching that God is perfectly good and holy and righteous. The Old Testament prophet Habakkuk said to God in Habakkuk 1:13, "Your eyes are too pure to look on evil. You cannot tolerate wrong." It was a good summary of the Bible's presentation of God. He's not morally indifferent. He's not morally mixed or compromised. He makes no errors in His timing or His plans. He is not weak or unable, but He is perfectly holy.

His holiness is indescribably high and great and weighty, and this is why God's offense at our sin is so great. This fever pitch of human rebellion was different in simple awfulness—God was bodily present—but not in kind. It was no different in kind from the sins you and I have committed against God this very week. And that's why, given the awful nature of sin, the punishment for sin would be so terrible. That's why a substitute was needed.

The second question: How could a substitute be given? How could there be a substitute in our place? God, the Creator and Judge, had decided that He would accept it. Indeed, He even seemed to be teaching that through the sacrifices of the Old Testament, the prophets, and now in Jesus' own teaching. One who was truly human yet truly God would come and obey for us, and take our punishment on Himself. We can see in our passage how full His obedience was, that He was willing to submit Himself to all of this. The Bible puts it this way: "God made him who had no sin to be sin for us, so that in him we might become the righteousness of God" (2 Cor. 5:21 NIV).

> GREG: This question you deal with here—How could a substitute be given?—is a pretty complex one. And you answer it, really, in one sentence. You say, essentially, that it can be so because God *decided* it would be so. Now I know there's a longer case than that for why that decision of God's was not unjust, and it has to do with our union with Christ. You didn't go into that at all. Why not?

> MARK: I'm a little reluctant to give a defense and a logical reason to explain something God has done, lest something be wrong with my reasoning or articulation of it and thereby bring God into disrepute. There are just certain places we come to in our faith where apologetics can actually become a little dangerous, and that's where I like the sheerness of "God the Judge has declared that He would accept a substitute."

Oh friends, particularly my religious friends here this morning, I hope you see here *clearly that not our zeal, not our tears and regrets, not our sincere emotional engagement, nothing* that we could do will ever undo the sins that we've already done. We have no way to have fellowship with the Holy God unless there could be a substitute. There must either be a substitute, or we are lost. We must have a Savior, and Jesus is the only Savior that there is. He is our hope. That's how there could be a substitute in our place.

That's why we need one and how there could be one, but there's still that question of, Why was a substitute given? Surely

God's perfections, His morality, His goodness could be fully shown throughout human history with never another thought taken for those who were in His image and rebelling against Him. He could simply exemplify His justice. Ah, but friends, see here in this substitute something of the extent of God's love! Christ was forsaken that we might never be.

Jesus had always had this in view. Even in Mark 2:20 He could refer to the time when the bridegroom Himself would be taken from them. He loved us this much. It was like we sang earlier in the song: "How deep the Father's love for us, how vast beyond all measure, that He should give His only son to make a wretch his treasure. How great the pain of searing loss. The Father turns his face away, as wounds, which mar the chosen one, bring many sons to glory."

Harvard law professor Bill Stuntz, who died last month of cancer, was an evangelical Christian. In a testimony at Park Street Church in Boston a couple of years ago, he quoted a line from *The Shawshank Redemption* that captures the point remarkably well. "Red describes Andy's escape, which required him to crawl through a long sewer line to get out of the prison complex. 'He crawled through a river of filth and came out clean on the other side.' That gets it right, I think. In times like this I see myself just as little as Andy, only I'm not the one who crawled through that nasty river. Someone else did it before me and for me."

Friends, at that point those Hollywood scriptwriters are echoing Isaiah. "We all, like sheep, have gone astray, each of us has turned to his own way; and the LORD has laid on him the inequity of us all. . . . It was the LORD's will to crush him and cause him to suffer. . . . He poured out his life on the death, and was numbered with the transgressors. For he bore the sin of many, and made intercession for the transgressors" (Isa. 53:6, 10, 12 NIV). How much he must love us in order to give and to be such a substitute for such people as you and me.

This is why Paul could write, "He who did not spare his own Son, but gave him up for us all—how will he not also, along with him, graciously give us all things?" (Rom. 8:32 NIV). Friends, Christ was forsaken so that we will never be.

I love the way one Puritan meditated on it. "Christ was all anguish that I might be all joy. Cast off that I might be brought in. Trodden down as an enemy that I might be welcomed as a friend. Surrendered to hell's worst that I might attain heaven's best. Stripped that I might be clothed. Wounded that I might be healed. A thirst that I might drink. Tormented that I might be comforted. Made ashamed that I might inherit glory. Entered darkness that I might have eternal life. Expired that I might forever live."

GREG: Don't know who this was, but it's a beautiful quote.

MARK: It's from the book *Valley of Vision*.

Friends, we see in Christ's death here the cost of our substitution. And . . .

Number three, we also see the dramatic suddenness of reconciliation. Where there had seemed to be no way to be reconciled to God, He made a way. By His death, Jesus made a way for sinners to come to a Holy God. We see in our passage the effect of Christ's punishment. Look again at verses 33–34 (NIV). "At the sixth hour darkness came over the whole land until the ninth hour. And at the ninth hour Jesus cried out in a loud voice, *'Eloi, Eloi, lama sabachthani?'*—which means, 'My God, my God, why have you forsaken me?'"

And then look down at verse 37. "With a loud cry, Jesus breathed his last. The curtain of the temple was torn in two, from top to bottom." Friends, Jim read for us earlier from Exodus, and you may remember that in Exodus the final plague before the angel of death came and effected the deliverance of God's people, the final plague was what? It was the plague of darkness. So here, the plague of darkness comes, right before Christ the Passover Lamb was sacrificed to deliver us. Darkness falls—darkness representing the judgment of God.

That loud cry in verse 37 marked His sudden death, and the suddenness of His death emphasizes the fact that Jesus' life didn't slowly drip out of Him, but that He gave it up willingly and deliberately. You remember He taught His disciples, "No one takes my life from me but I lay it down of my own accord." That loud cry there in verse 37, I assume from John's Gospel, is Christ's final statement. "It is finished." And when He uttered those words, "It is finished," God was once again creating by His word, speaking a new creation into existence.

In Exodus 26, God had commanded the people to make a veil, to separate the most holy place where the ark of the covenant was, with a mercy seat, from everything else. This curtain had the function of separating off the Holy God from unholy people, and that meant all the people—even the priests, even the *high* priests. The Lord told Moses, in Leviticus 16, to tell his brother, the high priest Aaron, not to come whenever he chooses through the veil into the most holy place or else he would die "because I appear in the cloud over the atonement cover."

In Hebrews 9 the author writes, "Now [Christ] has appeared once for all time at the end of the ages to do away with sin by the sacrifice of himself" (v. 26 NIV). Just as man is destined to die once and after that to face judgment, so Christ was sacrificed once to take away the sins of many people. Friends, as a dramatic witness to this new creation of sins forgiven, and to the fact that the last and greatest sacrifice had been offered, we see in verse 38 that "the curtain of the temple was torn." The whole sacrificial system of the Old Testament had been put in place to teach us that we needed forgiveness, not to bring about our forgiveness.

GREG: I thought your pulling together of the suddenness
of Jesus' death and the tearing of the veil was wonderful.
It's happening all at the same time.

All these sacrifices functioned kind of like airport runway lights,
just to direct our eyes to the right place. Nobody was going to fly on
them. It was never going to bring forgiveness, but it kept our eyes
directed right there, to see when the real thing would happen. It, as it
were, catechized and trained the people for centuries, trained them
to realize that there would be certain realities—forgiveness and
reconciliation—that would involve atonement, and atonement for sin
would involve sacrifice and blood and death. They also taught us that
the answer would come from outside of ourselves. Friends, all that
and more is going on in all of these sacrifices in the Old Testament,
but they never forgave sins. But that taught the people, ingrained
it deep in their understanding that sin involves death. Atonement
involves sacrifice.

GREG: The runway lights illustration was a little strange.
You say nobody actually uses them, but of course they do.
Planes land right on top of those lights.

MARK: I see what you're saying. . . . Of course I was moving so fast people probably didn't have time to figure out
the illogicality of my illustrations!

GREG: Yep, and looking at transcripts lets us be more
picky! I imagine people got the point.

And friends, that's what's going on here. What does Paul write
in Galatians 3: "Christ redeemed us from the curse of the law by
becoming a curse for us for it is written, 'Cursed is everyone who is
hung on a tree'" (v. 13 NIV). You see, the religious leaders, they had
it right. They had it right in the sense of thinking that Christ was
cursed. But they were wrong to think that they weren't, just because

they'd never hung on a tree. They had sinned against God. They misunderstood why Christ was cursed, but God's Word tells us that He was cursed for us. What He was doing was reconciling us through His blood shed on the cross. First Peter 3:18: "For Christ died for sins once and for all, the righteous for the unrighteous, to bring you to God" (NIV). You see, in Adam's and in our own lives, we have sinned away life and God and all, but now our trials, which began at another tree, would end decisively at this tree—the true tree of life.

Hebrews 13: "The high priest carries the blood of animals into the most holy place as a sin offering, but the bodies are burned outside the camp. And so Jesus also suffered outside the city gate, to make the people holy through his own blood. Let us, then, go to Him outside the camp, bearing the disgrace He bore, for we do not have an endearing city, but we are looking for the city that is to come."

Friends, you realize we gather each Sunday as a waiting party. We gather to wait, to encourage each other in waiting. We don't gather for ritual and sacrifice. That would be to confuse us. But ritual and sacrifice has all been done with the great sacrifice of Jesus Christ. No, we gather to rejoice and celebrate because of the one sacrifice made once for all time—we gather because Christ has made this sacrifice and by so doing has made a way for us, through His death, to be truly and forever reconciled to God.

Number four, we see the wideness of God's grace. Because of Jesus' death, God's grace would flow widely and surprisingly. Now I want to be very simple and brief, but I do want us just to note how the passage we read ends. You know, Jesus had taught that if anyone wants to be first he must be the very last and the servant of all, and many who are first will be last, and last first. And so we see something of that here, even in the cross. We see the extent of His grace.

You know, in the first century women were often thought less of than men, and yet here, when all the men, including even the religious leaders, had rejected Him, and even His own disciples had betrayed and denied and deserted Him, who would be the faithful witnesses of it all? These women. Look at verses 40–41: "Some women were watching from a distance. Among them were Mary Magdalene, Mary the mother of James the younger and of Joses and Salome. In Galilee these women had followed him and cared for his needs. Many other women who had come up with him to Jerusalem were also there" (NIV).

Why were their names recorded? By AD 60, when this is being written down, these women were monuments of the faith. These ladies, whom some of them may have actually known, had been witnesses to the central fact of human history—certainly the central fact of the Christian faith—and they were remembered and revered. Thank God for faithful women. How many churches in this country owe absolutely nothing to men because of their unfaithfulness and their worldliness and their attachment only to other things? And yet the women, faithfully, almost alone, continue on. How many of us, in our own lives, first heard the gospel from a faithful sister in Christ? Many of us.

> GREG: I thought it was interesting here that—when you're bringing the whole thing to a conclusion—you make the point about women. Do you think that messed up the momentum? I think it's a good point, but you've been meditating on all these glorious truths about salvation, and then you . . . appreciate the women in your church.

> MARK: Awww, I don't know. That's a good question, man. I think what I was trying to do there was just to show the wideness of God's mercy.

> GREG: The unexpectedness of it.

> MARK: Yea, it's just striking that all the male religious leaders were rejected, and there were the women, often

thought less of, who were the faithful witnesses. I don't know.

GREG: Well, it's obviously a good and true point, and it wasn't a long application. It was just kind of a detour from the main point.

And the nations, too, would come to know God. You see that in verse 39. It's this kind of down payment on the great outpouring of God's grace that was about to reach out to the nations, when all of the powerful and respected, and even the passersby of God's own people were rejecting Jesus, look who was presented as confessing the truth about Him: a Gentile occupying soldier.

Look at verse 39: "When the centurion, who stood there in front of Jesus heard his cry and saw how he died, he said, 'Surely this man was the Son of God!'" (NIV). Mark had begun his Gospel back in 1:1, saying, "The beginning of the gospel about Jesus Christ, the Son of God" (NIV). Now, as Mark nears his conclusion, who leads the way in turning the reader's attention to the crucial question, Who is Jesus? and even to the right answer? This Roman centurion.

The centurion would have been standing there to make sure no one tried to save the people who were being crucified. That happened sometimes, and so Rome learned to leave the soldiers there until the people actually died. By "Son of God" he may simply have meant something like, "I can't understand what's going on here. This is amazing. This guy is something more than human, like a divine being." But why would he draw this conclusion?

Well, there may be a number of reasons. One, the darkness you see up there in verse 33. And I think, also, as one who probably had witnessed a great many crucifixions, that loud cry would have been amazing. Someone dying of crucifixion would be asphyxiating. They would be all stuffed up. They could moan, but they couldn't make articulate words, certainly not many of them, and certainly not loudly. And if they did, it showed it must be a long time before they were going to die.

But friends, not here. Jesus makes this loud cry. He articulates words. He's understood. What power could explain this? In this centurion's confession we can see a foreshadowing of the fulfillment of God's ancient promise to Abraham, that through his offspring all the peoples on the earth would be blessed. And so the blessings would begin to flow at the foot of the cross, even then, in the moment of His death.

Again, Psalm 22:27: "All the ends of the earth will remember and turn to the LORD, and all the families of the nations will bow down before him" (NIV). In Daniel's vision we see that the Son of Man was given authority, glory, and sovereign power. All peoples, nations, and men of every language worshipped Him, and this is exactly what we see in Revelation 7: "There before me was a great multitude that no one could count, from every nation, tribe, people and language, standing before the throne and in front of the Lamb. They were wearing white robes and were holding palm branches in their hands, and they cried out, in a loud voice, 'Salvation belongs to our God, who sits on the throne, and to the Lamb'" (vv. 9–10 NIV).

You see how the cross becomes His throne and how the lamb has before Him, not just this one Roman centurion but now countless thousands upon thousands of people who are crying out the truth about Him saving others. He did not save Himself so that He could save others—save us. God's grace is surprising.

Christians, are you surprised that God saved you, or have you known about it so long it doesn't surprise you anymore? It should surprise you. If you knew yourself better, it would surprise you. It's surprising that God would save any of us. Friend, if you're here today and you're not a Christian, I want you to understand what Jesus did here. He made possible your salvation, if you would repent of your sins and trust in Him. Why would you not do that?

"God raised Him from the dead," we read in Romans 4, "for our justification" (see vv. 24–25). He signed, as it were, all the claims Jesus made, and we are here at Capitol Hill Baptist Church, eight hundred strong, testify to you that this is true. We are men and women from every walk of life, and our lives have all been changed by Jesus Christ. We would love to talk to you about what He can do in your life, the forgiveness He has, the power to change. You see something here of the wideness of God's grace in Christ.

> GREG: This is a wonderful appeal here to non-Christians to repent and believe. Do you do that in every sermon?

> MARK: Oh, I don't know. I certainly mean to, but I don't know if I do it every time.

Friends, we began by thinking about the oddness of Christianity, due in no small part to the oddness of what our passage today contains. We come expecting Jesus to be great, to be revered, to be strong, to be the master of His fate, the captain of His soul. You come expecting Jesus to be calm and composed. You come with all these expectations. And what you find is Jesus rejected and mocked, crying out in pain and anguish, unable to save Himself.

And yet, when we come to look at this strange, surprising picture more closely, we begin to find how horrible our sin is, and how it was paid for by Him, the substitute for all of us who will turn from our sins and trust in Him. He is the one who can reconcile us all to God. No matter what state we find ourselves in today, we heed His call.

Here's the way one nineteenth-century pastor reflected on the strangeness of Christ and His treatment here.

> When Christ uttered in the judgment hall of Pilate the remarkable words, "I am a king," he pronounced a sentiment fraught with unspeakable dignity and power. His enemies might deride His pretentions and express their

mockery of His claim by presenting Him with a crown of thorns, a reed, and a purple robe, and nailing Him to the cross, but in the eyes of unfallen intelligences, He was a king. A higher power presided over that derisive ceremony and converted it into a real coronation. That crown of thorns was, indeed, the diadem of empire. That purple robe was the badge of royalty. That fragile reed was the symbol of unbounded power, and that cross, the throne of dominion, which shall never end.

Friend, after thinking through all of this, does Christianity still seem odd to you? It should. It's so strange, it's unique. As John Piper recently observed, there was only one person God ever treated worse than He deserved, and that was Jesus, and He did it all for us, to bring us to God.

GREG: You didn't have much of a conclusion to this sermon. And you've been known to have five or six conclusions!

MARK: Very brief, yeah.

GREG: It tied back into the intro, but it was two or three sentences and done! Were you feeling time there? Or was it just short?

MARK: Because of the central message of the passage, I just thought it was clear and that I probably didn't need to say much more.

Let's pray together.

Lord, we are amazed at Your love for us. We pray that You would help us to understand more and more of our own sin and of Your amazing provision for us in Christ. Drive us out of ourselves and our own self-confidence and into the love of the Lord Jesus. We pray for our good and for Your eternal glory, in Jesus' name, Amen.

> GREG: It's a very good sermon, and an amazing text. Like you said in the sermon, you're here at the white hot center of biblical theology. So it was a beautiful sermon, and you were very passionate throughout.

> MARK: How could you not be with that passage?

Conclusion

———⬥———

A few years ago I (Mark) was reading biographies of both Albert Schweitzer (author of *The Quest for the Historical Jesus*) and Martyn Lloyd-Jones at the same time, and I was struck by the contrast between the two men.

Schweitzer, of course, left his theological training to pursue a medical degree and become a doctor in Africa. He wanted, he said, "to become one day the doctor whom these poor creatures needed."[20] Perhaps it was his uncertainty about the historical Jesus and the full-orbed meaning of his teaching that led him there, but he seemed throughout his life to have less faith in words and more in deeds. Schweitzer ultimately ended his life as a theologically trained doctor.

Lloyd-Jones, on the other hand, followed an almost exactly opposite path, leaving the practice of medicine in Harley Street to become a preacher in Wales. You could say that Lloyd-Jones had less faith in human deeds and more in God's Word. He was tired, he once said, of stitching people up just so they could go back out and continue to sin. Lloyd-Jones's certainty of the limitedness of medical help in dealing with human problems ultimately led him to the certainty of the gospel, and ultimately he ended life as a medically trained preacher.

A reporter for London's *Evening Standard* newspaper conducted an interview with Lloyd-Jones in April 1939: "'Why did you give up medicine for preaching?' I asked him. He looked at me searchingly, and, after a second's hesitation, replied: 'Because I became more interested in people than in their diseases.'"[21] As the doctor said in his famous lectures on *Preaching and Preachers*, "I would say without any hesitation that the most urgent need in the Christian Church today is true preaching; and as it is the greatest and most urgent need in the Church, it is obviously the greatest need of the world also."[22]

That is the privilege of preaching. We who proclaim God's Word are charged with proclaiming the only true message of salvation the world will ever know. We teach God's people, for whom Jesus died, and we call men and women to faith in Him, repentance from their sins, and salvation for all eternity. Yes, the work is hard. It is emotionally, physically, and even spiritually draining sometimes. But it is also a high privilege, one we should accept from our Lord's hand with humility, gratitude, and a determination to do it with all our hearts.

There is, however, peril in the call to preach as well. James puts the matter as plainly as anyone could: "Not many of you should become teachers, my brothers, for you know that we who teach will be judged with greater strictness" (James 3:1). And the author of Hebrews says that leaders in the church labor "as those who will have to give an account" (Heb. 13:17). Those are sobering words, and they remind us of the weight of what we do. Brothers, never take the privilege of preaching lightly.

Never forget what you do when you stand in the pulpit. You proclaim the words of God; you call men and women to salvation. You declare the glory of the Savior, Jesus Christ.

Notes

1. Nigel Tomm, *The Blah Story*, 23 volumes (Charleston, SC: BookSurge Publishing, 2007–2008).

2. E. C. Broome, "Ezekiel's Abnormal Personality," *Journal of Biblical Literature* 65 (1946), 277–92.

3. See, for example, Mark Dever and Michael Lawrence, *It Is Well: Sermons on Atonement* (Wheaton, IL: Crossway, 2009).

4. See Mark Dever's chapter in *Give Praise to God*, edited by Philip Graham Ryken, Derek W. H. Thomas, and J. Ligon, III Duncan (Phillipsburg, NJ: P & R Publishing, 2003).

5. James Reid, *Memoirs of the Westminster Divines*, vol. 2 (Carlisle, PA: Banner of Truth, 1983), 196.

6. Thomas Watson, *Heaven Taken by Storm* (Grand Rapids, MI: Soli Deo Gloria Ministries, 2003), 17.

7. Don Carson, ed., *Worship by the Book* (Grand Rapids, MI: Zondervan, 2002), 100.

8. Jonathan Leeman, *The Surprising Offense of God's Love* (Wheaton, IL: Crossway, 2009).

9. Bill McKibbens, "The Christian Paradox: How a faithful nation gets Jesus wrong," *Harper's Magazine* (August 2005), 34.

10. See Westminster Directory of Public Worship: Discussed by Mark Dever and Sinclair Ferguson (Christian Focus Publications, 2009).

11. "I confess that I frequently sit hour after hour praying and waiting for a subject, and this is the main part of my labor." Charles Spurgeon, *Lectures to My Students* (New York: Sheldon and Co., 1836), 136, 146.

12. The sermons have been reprinted in modern times. See Joseph Caryl, *Practical Observations on Job*, 12 volumes (Spring Lake, MI: Dust and Ashes Publications, 2001).

13. Iain Murray and David Martyn Lloyd-Jones, *The First Forty Years, 1899–1939* (Carlisle, PA: Banner of Truth, 1982), 147.

14. William Perkins, *The Art of Prophesying* (Carlisle, PA: Banner of Truth, 1996), 56–63.

15. D. Martyn Lloyd-Jones, *Romans: An Exposition of Chapters 3:20–4:25* (Carlisle, PA: Banner of Truth, 1998), xii.

16. From Baxter's poem, "Love Breathing Thanks and Praise."

17. Marcus Loane, *Makers of Puritan History* (Carlisle, PA: Banner of Truth, 2009), 190.

18. John Piper, *Counted Righteous in Christ* (Wheaton, IL: Crossway, 2002), 22–23.

19. P. J. King, "Capitol Hill: Late at Night," http://www.pillarontherock.com/2010/06/capitol-hill-late-at-night.html.

20. Hugh T. Kerr and John M. Mulder, *Famous Conversions* (Grand Rapids, MI: Eerdman's, 1994), 193.

21. Murray and Lloyd-Jones, *The First Forty Years,* 372.

22. D. Martyn Lloyd-Jones, *Preaching and Preachers* (Grand Rapdis, MI: Zondervan, 1972), 9.